SECOND EDITION

THE
EDUCATED
LISTENER

A New Approach
to Music Appreciation

BY JAREN S. HINCKLEY
BRIGHAM YOUNG UNIVERSITY

cognella® | ACADEMIC
PUBLISHING

Bassim Hamadeh, CEO and Publisher

Kassie Graves, Director of Acquisitions

Jamie Giganti, Senior Managing Editor

Jess Estrella, Senior Graphic Designer

Kristina Stolte, Senior Field Acquisitions Editor

Natalie Lakosil, Licensing Manager

Allie Kiekhofer and Kaela Martin, Associate Editors

TABLE OF CONTENTS

This book would not have been possible without the help of my friend and former student, Abigail Tippetts. Her editing skills, musical knowledge, and sense of humor were invaluable.

INTRODUCTION

THIS TEXTBOOK IS DESIGNED TO AID ANYONE—REGARDLESS OF musical knowledge—in developing skills needed for creatively and intelligently discussing and listening to music. By learning about the musical genres, forms, and techniques used by composers of Western classical music, you will gain a greater understanding of and appreciation for the art of music. You will become an educated listener.

In order to increase your musical knowledge effectively and quickly, here are some suggestions:

Use the text wisely:

This text is a giant glossary. Entries include a basic definition followed by a more detailed explanation. If you encounter a word that you do not understand, it is likely explained somewhere else in the text. Referring to the index will lead you to the correct information.

Ask questions:

At times, you may not understand something you hear on the radio, something you read in CD liner notes, in a program, or something the conductor or performer says prior to a performance. If this happens, ASK! Ask a musically knowledgeable friend. Ask a music instructor. Refer to this book! Don't be discouraged if you have a steep learning curve when it comes to grasping these new concepts. Do not be embarrassed to ask questions; asking leads to learning.

Listen to classical music:

Find out if you have a local classical radio station. If you're unsure, search online using the name of your city and "classical radio" as the keywords and see what comes up. Another option is listening on the Internet. Many classical radio stations have live streaming or an app that allows you to listen to that station online or on your smartphone. Once you have found a station or online source, you can immediately begin to increase your musical knowledge by paying attention to the things the announcer says about the music. Pandora.com, Rhapsody.com, Naxos.com, and iTunes are a few of the online programs, apps, and websites that can help you increase your listening opportunities. Some of these programs require a subscription fee, but others are free.

Attend musical events:

Every large city and many small towns have professional or community orchestras, performing arts centers that host chamber music concerts and other artistic events. Most universities have student and faculty recitals throughout the year—and many are free of charge. Whatever the venue, attend them! When you attend events like these, get a program and read it. Programs list the pieces to be performed, and many programs also contain program notes explaining various details about each piece on the program. You will learn a lot about music and its terminology by doing this simple thing.

Avoid snap judgments:

A lot of people make statements like "I hate opera" because at one time they had an initial negative reaction to it. If you give different styles of classical music multiple chances, you will discover that you like certain performers and composers better than others, but you'll never know what you like until you start listening. For example, I used to dislike opera, but after listening to examples of opera through various classes and performances, I discovered that there were certain operas (and certain composers) that I truly enjoyed. I am now much more willing to explore different genres and I learn something each time I do. My life is much richer as a result of my exposure to music—all kinds of music.

SUGGESTIONS FOR INSTRUCTORS

The primary purpose of introductory music history classes is to help students develop a love and understanding of classical music. Every instructor has his/her own unique approach to teaching. This text:

- is designed to help instructors pick and choose concepts they feel are most important to teach.
- focuses on the genres and forms that students are most likely to encounter at concerts, on the radio, at church services, and throughout their lives.
- does not attempt to cover all facets of music history; it presents the main genres, forms, styles, techniques, and basic information about the best-known composers from each time period.

The composer lists found at the end of each section are to provide both instructor and student a myriad of study options.

Text layout:
It is not necessary to proceed chapter by chapter. Maybe you will want to start with the Contemporary Era and work backwards; perhaps you prefer to skip the Middle Ages and the Renaissance; or you may want to organize your class by genre. This text is designed for flexibility so you can choose which topics to focus on and in what order you will proceed. If you prefer to teach a particular form in conjunction with a particular genre (found in a different chapter), by all means, do it! For example, I may want to teach ground bass in conjunction with the genre of opera. In that case, I would assign students to read about Baroque opera in one chapter and ground bass in another.

Reading assignments:
Because this text is essentially a large glossary, you can teach using a variety of approaches. Some professors prefer to introduce students to concepts in class and then assign readings that follow up and reinforce the knowledge gained. Others prefer to have the students read in advance so class time can be spent listening to music and discussing concepts that have already been studied. Others do a mix of both. Be creative!

Listening examples:

Because of the diversity of resources available to students and the lack of flexibility involved with sticking to a specific set of CDs, I have chosen to not provide a CD set with this textbook. This gives you the flexibility and freedom to create your own listening playlists using whatever online resources you have at your disposal. Most university libraries have subscriptions to online listening libraries such as Naxos, Classical Music Library, or Music Online, to name a few. These online services allow faculty to create listening lists with more flexibility than ever before. This text offers suggested listening for each genre and composer, but individual instructors should still create personalized listening lists geared directly to the topics being taught.

Listening charts:

In addition, most textbooks have listening charts that the students can follow along with as they listen. Because this text relies on individual instructors' personalized playlists for the listening examples, there is no way to include second-by-second listening charts. This should not be a problem; students learn material and retain it more deeply by being provided with a general chart of a particular form (like ritornello, sonata, or fugue) to follow along with the assigned listening. You may want to consider having students listen together in a "study group" setting to ensure that, through their collective intelligence, they succeed. The professor can then follow up at the next class session to see how students fared. Alternatively, individual professors can provide his/her own listening charts with a play-by-play to help the students in their at-home listening.

Assignments:

Numerous studies have shown that students learn through discussion, experience, and application. At the end of most entries are "Further Investigation" assignments and "Suggested Listening." These are intended for use either in class to facilitate discussion, or as assignments for students to complete between class sessions or as a follow-up or prelude to class instruction.

As the author of this text, it is my hope that you will find this a fun and new way of teaching introductory music history. It provides freedom for you to teach the topics you want to teach using the listening examples you want to use.

The future patrons of classical music are in your hands—help them become educated listeners and music lovers!

SECTION 1
PRELUDE

The history of music—its composers, its compositions, its forms and genres—is rich, vast, and exciting. In any study of the history of music, it is very helpful to understand basic music terminology. This section covers the basics of music, such as rhythm, tempo, and dynamics; the instruments and voice types used in music; and the most common ensembles of music, such as choirs, bands, and orchestras.

In addition, this section will help listeners get the most out of attending concerts by developing certain knowledge and skills that will make their experiences attending live productions of music much more fulfilling. Among the skills discussed are knowing when to clap, knowing how to decipher the material contained in the printed program, and knowing how to meet the current expectations of behavior while attending classical music concerts.

CHAPTER

ONE

Components of Music

HISTORICAL TIME PERIODS

Musicologists and historians determine time periods in a number of ways. In general, they take into account the stylistic, artistic, and musical characteristics that are most popular and common in any given time period and come up with a name for it. For the most part, these names were applied to these time periods—with the benefit of hind-sight—long after the time period ended.

The Middle Ages	450–1450
The Renaissance	1400–1600
The Baroque Era	1600–1750
The Classical Era	1750–1830
The Romantic Era	1810–1910
The Twentieth Century	1900–2000
The Contemporary Era	1960–present day

THE BASICS

Pitch

A **pitch** is a sound created by vibrations. More specifically, pitch refers to how high or low a particular sound is. If the vibration is fast, the pitch will be high; if it is slow, the pitch will be low. In string instruments, the sound is produced by the vibrating strings; in the human voice, by the vibrating vocal cords; and in brass and woodwind instruments, by the vibrating reed, lips, or column of air.

Note

A **note** is a specific pitch. Notes have letter names—A through G, for instance, is the basic music alphabet. Oftentimes, people use the words pitch and note interchangeably.

Chord

A **chord** is two or more notes played at the same time. There are certain kinds of chords that sound more normal to our Western ears, for instance the major triad. Sing "Do-Mi-Sol" to hear the three notes used in a major triad.

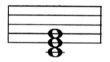

Consonance/Dissonance

Consonance is when music features notes that sound nice together—no real sense of discord or tension. Consonant moments sound conclusive or at rest.

Dissonance is when music features notes that don't sound nice together—there is a sense of discord or tension. Dissonant moments sound transitional or uneasy.

While these are certainly subjective judgments, when one note is sounded at the same time as another note, the listener has an immediate sense of dissonance or consonance.

Many composers choose to use dissonance sparingly, allowing brief moments of tension to develop before they resolve to a consonance. Other composers use dissonance non-stop because they want the listener to feel unsettled for the entire piece of music. Still other composers and listeners find the effect of dissonance to be enjoyable rather than unsettling.

Interval

An **interval** is the distance between any two pitches. These are the main intervals:

Minor second: A dissonant interval. To hear a minor second, play any key on the piano and then the very next key (regardless of color) or sing the first two notes of the *Jaws* theme. This is also known as a half step.

Major second: A mildly dissonant interval. Sing the first two notes of a major scale ("Do-Re") and you'll hear a major second. This is also known as a whole step.

Minor third: A slightly dissonant interval. Sing the first two notes of "Greensleeves" (also known as "What Child Is This?").

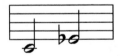

Major third: A consonant interval. Sing "Do-Mi" or the first two notes of "I Heard the Bells on Christmas Day."

Perfect fourth: A consonant interval. Sing "Do-Fa" or the first two notes of "Here Comes the Bride."

Tri-tone (also known as an augmented fourth, a diminished fifth, or "the devil's interval"): A very dissonant interval. Sing the first two syllables of "Maria" from *West Side Story* or sing the words "The Simpsons," at the start of the television theme song—the first two syllables ("The Simp-") make a tri-tone.

Perfect fifth: An extremely consonant interval. Sing "Do-Sol" or "Twinkle Twinkle Little Star"—when you move from the first twinkle to the second twinkle, you have sung a perfect fifth.

Minor sixth: A somewhat dissonant interval. Sing the first two notes of "Close Every Door," from *Joseph and the Amazing Technicolor Dreamcoat*. Or, sing the first four notes of Scott Joplin's "The Entertainer"; the third and fourth notes are a minor sixth (and so are the fifth and sixth notes and the seventh and eighth notes).

Major sixth: A consonant interval. Sing "Do-La" or the first two notes of "My Bonnie Lies Over the Ocean" or the first two notes of the NBC jingle.

Minor seventh: A dissonant interval. Sing the first two notes of "Somewhere" from *West Side Story*. In the main theme of the original *Star Trek* television series, the first two notes that are sung (by the female voice) form a minor seventh.

Major seventh: A very dissonant interval. Sing "Do-Ti" or the first two notes of the chorus of "Take On Me" by the band a-ha. Or, if you are familiar with 80s television theme songs, the first two notes of the theme song to *Fantasy Island*.

Octave: The most consonant interval. Sing "Do-Re-Mi-Fa-Sol-La-Ti-Do." The first and last "Do" create an octave. Or you can sing the first two notes of the chorus of "Somewhere Over the Rainbow" from *The Wizard of Oz*.

Unison: A unison is the same note sung or played by more than one person. (It is technically not a true "interval" since there is no distance between the two notes.)

Scale

A **scale** is a succession of whole-step and half-step intervals that sound normal or logical to our Western ears.

There are three main types of scales used in Western music today—**major**, **minor**, and **chromatic**.

Major scale: A major scale is created by playing the succession of whole steps (W) and half steps (H) indicated on the illustration below. Sing "Do-Re-Mi-Fa-Sol-La-Ti-Do" and you will have sung a major scale.

W   W   H   W   W   W   H

<u>Minor scale</u>: A minor scale is created by playing a different succession of whole and half steps.

<u>Chromatic scale</u>: A chromatic scale is created by playing only half steps—no whole steps.

By following the above successions of intervals, anyone can play these scales starting on any note.

Melody

A **melody** is a succession of notes—any succession of notes. Composers choose which pitches and intervals they want to use in their melody. In very general terms, the melody is the catchy, hummable part of a piece of music.

Because melody is such a general term, there are other terms that are helpful in describing a particular piece of music.

<u>Phrase</u>: A **phrase** is a short melody that, if you were singing it, would feel quite natural to take a breath at the end. For instance, "Jingle Bells, Jingle Bells, Jingle all the way [breath]. Oh what fun it is to ride in a one-horse open sleigh [breath]." Or for a slower example, "Silent Night, [breath] Holy Night, [breath], all is calm, [breath], all is bright [breath]."

<u>Motive</u>: A **motive** is a short succession of notes that is used throughout a piece of music to create a sense of unity within the piece. Motives can be melodic or rhythmic. One of the most famous motives in music history is the first four notes of Beethoven's *Symphony No. 5* (dum-dum-dum-DUUUUUUM).

<u>Theme</u>: A **theme** is similar to a motive but longer. The opening clarinet solo in Gershwin's *Rhapsody in Blue* is a good example. It is heard right at the beginning of the piece, played by the clarinet, then it comes back time and time again played by various instruments within the orchestra.

Harmony

Harmony is musical material that enhances or supports the melody. Any other notes that occur at the same time as a melody can be considered part of the harmony. For instance, in most hymns or music sung by choirs, it is customary to have four-part harmony—the soprano line (the melody line), the alto line, the tenor line, and the bass line. Aside from the melody line, the other three parts are considered harmony. (Harmony features notes lined up vertically on the page, while melody features notes arranged in succession horizontally.)

STRUCTURAL ELEMENTS

Key/Tonality/Atonality

A **key** is an organizing principle within a composition. Key is determined by the first note in the scale; in other words, if a scale begins on the note called C and a piece is composed using the notes in the C scale, we would say that that piece is written in the key of C.

Every note within a scale has a functional name as labeled here:

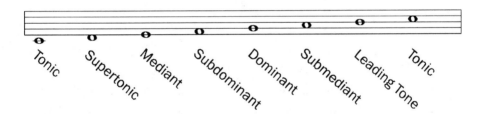

The first note of each scale is called the **tonic**. Turn on a piece of music and listen for a moment, then start to hum the note that seems to be the most prominent overall. You will likely find that you are humming the tonic. The tonic acts as a homing signal that draws us in throughout the music and provides a sense of conclusiveness at the end of a piece. The tonic is most obvious in the bass line. You may notice that occasionally, when you are humming the tonic, it goes away and you can't find it for a few moments. The bass line has most likely moved to the subdominant or dominant notes briefly before returning to the tonic. The word that describes what happens when a piece of music moves from one key to another is **modulation**. The composer modulates the piece from one key to another.

Tonality is when a piece of music has a distinct tonic. The tonic may be present for the entire piece, or a composer may choose to modulate the piece to other keys, each having its own tonic. We label this music as tonal. When you see a title of a piece such as *Sonata in E minor*, you know that E is the tonic.

Atonality is when a piece of music avoids maintaining a tonic. Atonal music is fairly dissonant.

Chord Progression/Cadence

A **chord progression** is the order in which a series of chords occurs. The harmony of most music relies on chords built upon various notes in a particular scale. Throughout history, certain chord progressions have developed that sound normal to our ears. For instance, think of the bass line at the start of "Summer Lovin'" from *Grease*. The bass line is T (tonic), T, S (subdominant), S, D (dominant), D, S, D, S, T with chords punctuating each note of the bass line—chords built on the tonic, subdominant, and dominant. This chord progression is used so consistently throughout history in thousands of pieces of music that it can easily be considered the most popular chord progression in Western music. Most pieces of music from the Classical Era, for example, end with a chord progression of T, S, D, D, T.

A **cadence** is the last few chords in a chord progression. Ending on the tonic chord provides a sense of conclusion. Cadences occur in music at the ends of phrases and at the end of the entire piece. Cadences at the ends of compositions often emphasize (repeat) the tonic numerous times to ensure that listeners feel a sense of conclusiveness.

Rhythm

Rhythm is how music occurs within time. At its most basic, rhythm is the succession of *durations* of notes. Some rhythms will feature repeated notes of the same duration, and some rhythms will feature notes with varied durations.

Beat

A **beat** is a regularly recurring pulse. Musical time is measured in beats. Turn on a rock song with a heavy drumbeat and see what effect it has upon you. Most likely you will start tapping your toe (or banging your head) in a regular, evenly spaced pulse. If you can do that, you have found the beat of the music.

Measure/Bar

A **measure** (or **bar**) is a unit of musical time. Measures are indicated in music by vertical bar lines that look like this:

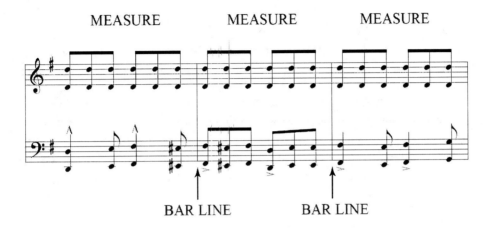

MEASURE   MEASURE   MEASURE

BAR LINE   BAR LINE

Meter

Meter is a pattern of regularly recurring accented beats and unaccented beats. There are many different types of meter:

Duple meter: Duple meter is a recurring pattern of one accented beat followed by one unaccented beat—heavy-light, heavy-light. Most marches are in duple meter. Here are some possible duple-meter indications (known as time signatures):

Triple meter: Triple meter is a recurring pattern of one accented beat followed by two unaccented beats—heavy-light-light, heavy-light-light. Waltzes and many other dances are in triple meter. Here are some possible triple-meter time signatures:

Quadruple meter: Quadruple meter is a recurring pattern of one accented beat followed by a light beat, then a somewhat heavy beat, and then a final light beat—heavy-light-somewhat heavy-light. This meter is also called common time because it is so prevalent in music. Listen to practically any pop song and you will likely hear common time. Here are some possible quadruple meter time signatures:

Compound meter: Compound meter is a recurring pattern of accented beats and unaccented beats that can be perceived as either duple or triple; and each beat can be subdivided into three beats. As an example of this, sing "Silent Night" much faster than you normally would—you'll find that it is in duple meter. Then sing it more slowly, the way it is normally sung, and you'll find that it can be perceived in a triple meter.

Si - lent night,   Ho - ly night,   All   is calm,   All   is bright.

Non-metrical: Some music has no regular recurring pattern of beats and, therefore, no meter. Gregorian chant, for example, is non-metrical.

Mixed meter: Mixed meter is when a piece of music has one meter for a certain amount of time, then shifts to another meter. These shifts can occur every single measure in a piece of music or can occur infrequently. Listeners might *perceive* pieces composed with mixed meter as non-metrical, but they are still metrical; the constant shifting just makes it more difficult to tap your toes as you listen.

Irregular meter: Irregular meter has an irregular number of beats per measure: for instance, five beats per measure, or seven, or eleven. If a meter isn't easily divisible by two or three, it is irregular.

Texture

Texture is the means by which melody, harmony, and rhythm are combined in a composition.

Monophony: The most basic texture, monophony, is found in music in which a single melody line has absolutely no harmony. Examples of **monophonic texture** in daily life include someone whistling a tune or singing in the shower.

Homophony: This texture is found in music in which a melody line is enhanced or supported by other musical material, usually chords. Examples of **homophonic texture** in daily life include hymns, most pop songs, and patriotic songs.

Polyphony: This texture is found in music in which there are two or more melodic lines that are equal (or practically equal) in importance. There are two main types of **polyphonic texture**:

> **Imitative polyphony** is when one melody line begins and then another melody begins shortly thereafter, imitating the first melody line. The second line might be higher or lower in pitch, or it might use exactly the same pitches as the initial melody, but because the individual entrances are staggered, they are identifiable as separate melodies. There can be as many melodies involved in imitative polyphony as the composer wants. Examples of **imitative polyphonic texture** in daily life include rounds (like "Row, Row, Row Your Boat") and fugues.

> **Non-imitative polyphony** is when there are two or more contrasting melody lines going on at the same time. Examples of **non-imitative polyphonic texture** include the kids' song "Fish and Chips and Vinegar" and "One Day More" from *Les Misérables* (where each character sings his/her own individual melody overlapping with the other characters' individual melodies).

Form

Form refers to the way a particular piece of music is laid out—a roadmap or blueprint that a composer can follow as he composes a particular piece of music. When diagramming form, letters are used to indicate repetition or contrast. Whatever the first section of music sounds like, it is labeled A; if that first section repeats, it is labeled A again. Or if it is contrasting material, it is labeled B. If another contrasting section occurs, it is labeled C.

As an example, sing "My Bonnie" and notice how it is diagrammed below:

A	My Bonnie lies over the ocean My Bonnie lies over the sea My Bonnie lies over the ocean Oh, bring back my Bonnie to me
B	Bring back, bring back Oh bring back my Bonnie to me, to me Bring back, bring back Oh bring back my Bonnie to me

The first part is very obviously a different melody from the second part.

Here's an example of a piece in ABA form: in other words, a piece in which the first section is repeated following a contrasting section. Sing this song aloud and pay attention to how the initial A melody repeats following the B melody.

A	Baa, baa, black sheep, have you any wool? Yes sir, yes sir, three bags full.
B	One for the master, one for the dame, One for the little boy who lives down the lane.
A	Baa, baa, black sheep, have you any wool? Yes sir, yes sir, three bags full.

Note: Diagramming music has nothing to do with the words and everything to do with the melody. In "Baa, Baa, Black Sheep," both A sections had the same words, but you could also sing the alphabet song and notice that even though the two A sections have different words, they should still be diagrammed with A, because they have the exact same melody.

This next example has no repetition of sections:

A	I've been working on the railroad all the live-long day. I've been working on the railroad just to pass the time away.
B	Can't you hear the whistle blowing, Rise up so early in the morn; Can't you hear the captain shouting, "Dinah, blow your horn!"
C	Dinah, won't you blow, Dinah, won't you blow, Dinah, won't you blow your horn? Dinah, won't you blow, Dinah, won't you blow, Dinah, won't you blow your horn?
D	Someone's in the kitchen with Dinah Someone's in the kitchen I know Someone's in the kitchen with Dinah Strummin' on the old banjo!

Most pop music and rock-and-roll songs follow a very basic pattern of verse, verse, chorus, verse, chorus—or, in other words, AABAB. Listen to your favorite pop songs and pay attention to the patterns of repetition and contrast. Occasionally, a section might repeat (A A, for example), but on the repeated part, the composer might have made small changes—not enough to obscure the relationship to the first

A, but enough to be noticeable. In these cases, a prime is added to the slightly altered section, like so: A A'.

Movement

A **movement** is a self-contained portion of music (with a beginning, middle, and end) that is part of a larger work. In the example below, the piece listed has a main title followed by four individual movements (indented). Each movement sounds like a complete piece of music. You might even feel like you ought to clap at the end of the first movement (especially if it is particularly exciting), but the first movement is not the end of the complete piece; you need to wait until all four movements are complete before you applaud.

Quintet in D minor, Op. 68, No. 3   Franz Danzi
     Andante sostenuto—Allegretto   (1763–1826)
     Andante
     Minuetto: Allegretto
     Finale: Allegro assai

Many music lovers feel that this rule about applause is silly, while others most vociferously defend the practice. In any event, the current concert-going etiquette is to wait until the end of the *entire* piece to applaud. When you attend concerts, follow along with the program to keep track of the movements so that you know when to applaud.

Score

Score is the word used to describe a printed piece of music. There are solo scores, chamber scores, vocal scores, and orchestral scores.

When studying music, it is very helpful to look at scores while you listen. To find scores, the easiest and quickest method is to search for the composer and title of the piece you are studying at the International Music Score Library Project's website (imslp.org). Most music libraries at universities also have a tremendous number of scores available.

Excerpt from a chamber music **score** by Franz Schubert (Piano Trio No. 2 in E-Flat Major, Op. 100, D. 929, mvt. II)

EXPRESSIVE MARKINGS

Expressive markings are words or symbols that provide guidance to the performer as to how to perform a piece of music. These markings indicate the mood, volume, or speed of the music.

Dynamics

Dynamics are descriptive markings or words printed in the music that indicate volume—how loud or how quiet. Because a lot of musical terms developed at a time when Italy was the artistic center of Europe, we use Italian words to describe dynamics. Dynamics are indicated with various symbols and abbreviations (below the printed notes).

ITALIAN TERM	ENGLISH TRANSLATION	SYMBOL OR ABBREVIATION USED TO INDICATE DYNAMIC
Pianississimo	Triple soft	**ppp**
Pianissimo	Double soft	**pp**
Piano	Soft	**p**
Mezzo-piano	Medium soft	**mp**
Mezzo-forte	Medium loud	**mf**
Forte	Loud	**f**
Fortissimo	Double loud	**ff**
Fortississimo	Triple loud	**fff**
Crescendo	Gradually get louder	**cresc.** or $<$ (this symbol is placed underneath a section of music and is as short or as long as the composer wants the crescendo to take place.)
Decrescendo or *Diminuendo*	Gradually get softer	**decresc.** or **dim.** or $>$
Subito	Suddenly	**sub.** This dynamic marking is only used in conjunction with a specific volume, like so: **sub. fff** or **sub. p**

Dynamics are only general terms. It is up to the individual performer to decide how loud or soft one dynamic is in relation to another dynamic.

Tempo

Tempo is the speed of music. Composers can indicate how fast or how slow a particular piece or section of a piece is by using tempo markings. These are generally in Italian, although other languages are occasionally used. They appear above the printed music at the beginning of the piece and whenever the composer changes the tempo within a piece of music. They also appear in the printed program at music performances, so it is helpful for you to have a working knowledge of these terms. Here is a chart showing the most commonly used tempo markings.

DESIRED SPEED OF MUSIC	TEMPO MARKINGS COMMONLY USED
Very slow	*Grave, Largo,* and *Lento*
Slow	*Adagio*
Somewhat slow	*Andante* (often translated as "at a walking pace")
Medium speed	*Moderato*
Somewhat fast	*Allegretto*
Fast	*Allegro* and *Vivace* (lively)
Very fast	*Presto*

As with dynamics, these terms are still quite general, so it is up to the individual performer to determine how fast or slow each tempo really is. Many composers try to be more specific by using certain modifiers in their tempo markings.

MODIFIER	WHAT IT MEANS	HOW IT MIGHT APPEAR IN CONJUNCTION WITH A TEMPO MARKING
Agitato	Agitated	*Allegro agitato*
Animato	Animated, with life	*Allegro animato*
Appassionato	With passion	*Allegro appassionato*
Assai	Very	*Allegro assai*
Cantabile	In a singing manner	*Allegretto cantabile*
Con brio	With vigor	*Allegro con brio*
Con fuoco	With fire	*Presto con fuoco*
Con moto	With motion	*Allegro con moto*
Espressivo	With expressiveness	*Andante espressivo*
Giocoso	With joy	*Allegro giocoso*
Grazioso	With gracefulness	*Allegro grazioso*
Maestoso	Majestic	*Allegro maestoso*
Molto	Much	*Molto allegro*
Non troppo	But not too much	*Allegro non troppo*

The above table is only a sample of the myriad possible terms used as modifiers. If you see a tempo marking that you've never seen before, try using basic knowledge of Latin-based languages (including English) to make educated guesses as to meaning. For instance, one can infer that *Presto furioso* means fast and furious or that *Andante sostenuto* means slow and sustained.

Here are other tempo markings that help guide performers in their music-making:

ITALIAN TERM	ENGLISH TRANSLATION	SYMBOL OR ABBREVIATION USED
Accelerando	Speeding up	**accel.**
Meno mosso	Less motion	**meno mosso**
Più mosso	More motion	**più mosso**
Poco a poco	Little by little	**poco a poco** This term is usually used in conjunction with another tempo marking: for instance, **poco a poco accelerando** would mean "little by little, speed up."
Rallentando or *Ritardando*	Slowing down	**rall.** or **rit.**

Composers can also indicate exact tempo by using metronome markings. A **metronome** is a time-indicating device that clicks or beeps a certain number of times per minute. As an example, if the metronome marking is ♩ = 60, the click would occur sixty times per minute—a relatively slow tempo. If the metronome marking is ♩ = 176 the click would occur 176 times per minute. On a traditional metronome, 40 is the lowest tempo and 208 is the fastest tempo.

DESCRIPTIVE TERMS

Tone Color/Timbre

Tone color or **timbre** (the terms are interchangeable) is the quality of sound of an instrument or voice. Tone color is affected by the way the sound vibrations are created. To describe tone color, use descriptive adjectives like smooth, harsh, nasal, mellifluous, or even toad-like. Sing the exact same pitch multiple times with a different timbre each time; for instance, sing a note with a nasal tone color, then sing the same note with a hollow tone color, then with a gravelly tone color.

Note: Sometimes people make the mistake of describing the mood of a piece when they're trying to describe tone color. Mood and tone color are two different concepts.

Genre

Genre is a word that essentially means the same thing as category. In music, a genre is a term that helps categorize a particular piece of music by characteristics it shares with other compositions.

It might be helpful to illustrate this concept using the world of film as an example. Within the many possibilities of types of films to watch, we find genres such as comedy, action, romance, horror, children's, and westerns. Every film in the western genre shares similar characteristics, the most obvious being that they all take place in the wild West and involve gunfights, horses, and saloons. Yet every western is also uniquely individual. So we use more specific titles within the genre to identify the specific films—*High Noon*, *True Grit*, and *The Wild Bunch* to name a few. Each of these films is easily recognized as a western, yet they are also unique.

It works the same way in the world of music. In music, *concerto* is a specific genre, or category of composition. Individual pieces of music within that genre have more specific titles to help them be identified more specifically than the general term of genre. As with a western-genre film, there are hundreds of concerti with unique characteristics and identifying factors with titles such as:

- *Marimba Concerto No. 1*
- *Piano Concerto No. 12 in A major, K. 414*
- *Brandenburg Concerto No. 3 in G major, BWV 1048*
- *The Butterfly Lovers Violin Concerto*

Another example: A genre that originated in the Catholic Church is called Mass. The Mass is a specific church service; it is also a musical genre that has developed and evolved through the centuries. Within the vast genre of Mass there are hundreds of masses identified more specifically with identifying titles such as:

- *Mass No. 3 in C major, Hob.XXII:5*
- *Mass No. 16 in C major, K. 317, "Krönungsmesse"*
- *Messe solennelle, Op. 16*
- *Mša glagolskaja (Glagolitic Mass), JW III/9*

At some point, you may be asked, "Do you like listening to concertos?" or "Do you enjoy the music of the Catholic Mass?" If you reply in the affirmative, you may be asked, "Which ones?" The person asking you questions has determined that you enjoy the genre of the concerto or the Mass, and now they want more specific titles.

Genre is quite a useful term and can be very broad or very specific. For example, in the world of music one *could* divide up all music that has ever existed into two rather large genres—1) art music and 2) pop music. These are *extremely* broad genres. Within each of these genres are hundreds of sub-genres. For instance, in the large genre of pop music, there are the sub-genres of R&B, bubble gum pop, country-western, hair metal, and grunge, to name a few; and within the large genre of art music there are hundreds of sub-genres such as concerto, sonata, symphony, string quartet, and piano trio.

Program Music/Absolute Music

Program music is music that is meant to tell a story or paint a picture in the head of the listener. **Absolute music** is music that is *not* meant to tell a story. It is music for music's sake.

Song/Piece/Work

A **song** is sung. Songs are usually quite short and are sung by a small number of people. For instance, most pop music can be referred to as songs. When a group sings "Happy Birthday" to a friend, it is a song. Occasionally a song can be sung by a very large group of people: for instance, "Take Me Out to the Ballgame" sung at a ballpark. It is incorrect to refer to a large-scale composition like Beethoven's *Symphony No. 9* or Verdi's *Aida* as a song.

The word **piece** is a handy catch-all term that can apply to all instrumental music *and* vocal music (including songs).

A **work** is a large-scale multi-movement (or multi-sectioned) piece of music such as an opera, an oratorio, a symphony, a song cycle, etc.

Pop Music/Art Music

Pop music is music that is "popular." Rock-and-roll, musical theatre, film music, and jazz are categories of popular music.

Art music is music that is artistic in intent. Classical music from the Middle Ages through the present day is considered art music.

Both terms are problematic. Labeling a piece of music as pop implies that it is not artistic; labeling a piece of music as art music implies that it is not popular. But neither of those implications is true or fair. Jazz, musical theatre, film music, and rock-and-roll all have artistic merit. And art music is indeed popular all over the world. For the purposes of this book, however, these terms will be used, with the understanding that pop music and art music are both popular AND artistic.

CHAPTER

TWO

Instruments and Ensembles

INSTRUMENTS OF ART MUSIC

Woodwind Instruments

For all woodwind instruments, pitch is changed by covering and uncovering holes in the body of the instrument and pressing on various keys and buttons.

Flute:

- **Flute**: Historically, the flute was made of wood; currently, flutes made of metal are standard. The sound is created by blowing across the top of a small opening. To understand how this makes a sound, blow across the top of a bottle.
- **Piccolo**: The piccolo is essentially a half-size flute. It is considerably smaller and plays at a higher pitch. Professional models are made of wood, although metal and resin models are also popular.
- **Alto flute**: This is a larger, and therefore lower, flute. It has a deeper, more-breathy tone color than the regular flute.

An artisan takes a break from work to play his flute (but with gloves on?).

Man in marching band playing the piccolo.

- There are also bass flutes and tenor flutes, but they are rarely used.

Oboe:

- **Oboe:** The oboe is made of dark wood and is played by blowing through a small double reed (two pieces of carefully shaped cane strapped back to back).
- **English horn:** The English horn is larger and longer than the oboe but appears fairly similar. It has a warmer and richer tone color and a lower range.

Clarinet:

- **Clarinet:** The clarinet is played by blowing through a mouthpiece to which is strapped a single-cane reed. It is made from the same wood as the oboe.
- **Bass clarinet:** This is a rather large clarinet that looks similar to a saxophone, although it is made of a dark wood and rests on the floor.
- **E-flat clarinet:** This is a quite small clarinet. It is high in pitch and has a shrill tone color.
- There are also alto clarinets, contrabass clarinets, and more.

Bassoon:

- **Bassoon:** The bassoon is a double-reed instrument much larger than the oboe and therefore has a lower pitch and a richer tone color.
- **Contrabassoon:** This is a huge bassoon that plays very low notes.

Members of the Symphony Society of New York (1917) pose with their instruments. From left to right, the English horn, the clarinet and the bassoon.

Oboe
Copyright © Depositpho-
tos/alenavlad

Saxophone
Copyright © Depositphotos/
ozaiachinn.

Bass clarinet
Copyright © Depositpho-
tos/Furtseff.

Saxophone:

- **Alto saxophone**: Although it is made of brass, the saxophone is a single-reed instrument and shares a similar fingering system with the rest of the woodwinds. This is the most commonly seen and heard saxophone, especially in jazz and pop music. The inventor of the saxophone intended for it to be a regular part of the standard orchestra. Although that never really caught on, hundreds of composers have composed art music repertoire for this instrument.
- There are also soprano, tenor, baritone, and contra-bass saxophones.

Other Woodwind Instruments:

- **Recorder**: The recorder is similar to early wood-flutes, but sound is produced by blowing through a whistle-type mouthpiece rather than by blowing across the top of a hole. Because of the focus on recorder in elementary schools, many people

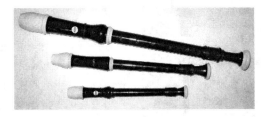

Recorders
Copyright in the Public Domain.

do not realize that the recorder is actually recognized as an important instrument in the world of art music. Recorder virtuosi of today continue to impress by

Trumpet

Horn

Trombone

performing concerti by Vivaldi, Corelli, Telemann, and other Baroque composers. The recorder can also be called the *blockflöte* and comes in many varieties, such as alto, tenor, and bass.

Brass Instruments

Brass instruments are made of metal tubing coiled into various shapes to allow for various tone colors. The length and width of tubing influence how high or low a particular instrument sounds. All brass instruments produce sound by the performer's buzzing lips pressed into a circular cup-shaped metal mouthpiece. Pitch is influenced by how fast or slow the lips are buzzing, assisted by the use of valves or a slide.

Trumpet:

- **Trumpet**: The trumpet has a bright, brassy tone color and uses valves (buttons) that open up passageways to different lengths of mostly cylindrical tubing.
- **Piccolo trumpet**: This is the highest trumpet used today. It was extremely popular in the Baroque Era. If you hear a piece of music with a really high trumpet, there is a good possibility that it was composed in the Baroque Era.
- There are also other trumpet-like instruments called the cornet and the flugelhorn.

Horn, or French Horn:

- The **horn** has the mellowest tone color of the brass family and is thus often referred to as an honorary woodwind. It has valves (spatula keys) similar to the trumpet but has a large bell at the end of the tubing into which the performer places the right hand to help influence pitch, volume, and tone color.
- **Mellophone**: This is basically a horn that has been shaped with the bell facing forward. It has a similar tone color to the horn and is used most frequently in marching bands.

Trombone:

- The **trombone** is similar in tone color to the horn but lower in pitch. Unlike the other brass instruments, the trombone changes pitch using a long slide to extend the tubing. This gives the trombone its unique ability to smear from one note to another smoothly. Some professional models have one or two valves to facilitate note changes.

• There are alto, tenor, and bass varieties.

Tuba:

• **Tuba**: This is the largest brass instrument standard in a typical orchestra. It has a large bell that points upward and uses valves to change pitch.

• **Sousaphone**: A tuba designed to be used in marching bands; the bell faces forward to project the sound more directly, and the tubing wraps around the performer for ease of carrying while marching.

Tuba

Detail from a painting—The Violinist—by Paolo Giovanni Bedini (1844–1924).

Viola

Cello

Double bass

String Instruments

The majority of the string family produces sound when a bow (made of horse hair) is drawn across four gut or synthetic strings to produce the vibrations. The right hand holds the bow; the left hand places fingers on the fingerboard to create different pitches. The strings can also be plucked (a technique called *pizzicato*). Because the bow can be drawn across more than one string at a time, string instruments can often play both melody and harmony at the same time. Playing two strings at once is a technique known as **double stops**. String players also use a technique known as *vibrato* in which the left hand wiggles back and forth, which causes a wavering pitch.

Violin:

- The **violin** is the smallest of the standard orchestral strings and is held under the chin. It can have a bright, thin tone color in its highest notes and a warm, mellow tone color in its lower notes.

Viola:

- The **viola** is slightly larger than the violin and has a warm, dark tone color.

Cello:

- Also referred to as a **violoncello**, this is a larger instrument that looks similar to the violin and viola, but instead of being held under the chin, it is placed on the floor between the legs of the performer. It has a lower pitch and a darker tone color than the viola.

Double-bass:

- This is the largest string instrument. Performers of the **double-bass** (also called string bass, upright bass, or bass) either stand or sit on a tall stool while playing.

Classical guitarist Dionysio Aguado (1784–1849).
Copyright in the Public Domain.

A drawing from 1827 of Olivia Dussek playing the harp.
Copyright in the Public Domain.

Other String Instruments:

These other instruments are considered string instruments because the sound produced is the result of vibrations of strings; these instruments are not bowed but are instead strummed or plucked.

- **Guitar:** The guitar has six strings and, although it is endemic in pop music, its origins are in art music; there is a vast art-music repertoire for the guitar.
- **Harp:** The harp has a large wood soundboard with up to 47 strings. Professional harps have seven pedals at the base that have three positions—natural, lowered, and raised—by which the performer can change keys. There are also less-complex harps for beginners and Celtic harps used mostly in folk music.

Percussion Instruments

A percussion instrument is any instrument in which the principal means of producing sound is by striking the instrument. Some percussion instruments are pitched, meaning they produce a specific note that can be matched on the piano keyboard, and others are un-pitched, meaning that the vibrations produced are not regular enough to create a specific pitch (stomp your foot and you will hear an un-pitched sound).

Cover of a timpani method book.

Marimba

- **Timpani**: A set of pitched instruments, also known as the kettledrums, timpani are placed in a half-circle of four to six separate drums of different sizes. Each timpani also has a foot pedal by which the performer can change pitch.
- **Glockenspiel**: Pitched. A glockenspiel is laid out with two rows of metal bars containing all the pitches of the chromatic scale. To strike the bars, performers use hard rubber or wood mallets.
- **Xylophone**: Pitched. The xylophone is extremely similar to a glockenspiel, but it has wood bars and is lower in pitch.
- **Vibraphone**: Pitched. Similar to a xylophone but much larger with metal tubes underneath each bar to help the sound resonate and ring. Inside each metal tube is a rotating disc that creates a regular vibrato effect. There is also a damper pedal to muffle the sound.
- **Marimba**: Pitched. The marimba is similar to the vibraphone but has wood bars and no rotating discs.
- **Chimes**: Pitched. Chimes are metal tubes that hang vertically from a frame and are struck at the top with a hammer. There is also a damper pedal.
- **Snare drum**: Un-pitched. A snare drum is a small drum struck with wood drum-sticks. There are metal springs, called snares, stretched out along the bottom of the drum, which create a rattle when the drum is struck. Think of the beginning

Chimes

Snare drum

of practically any military march—usually the first sounds you hear are produced by the snare drum.

- **Tambourine**: Un-pitched. The tambourine is a wooden hoop with metal discs loosely inset all around the hoop to rattle against each other when struck.
- **Castanets**: Un-pitched. Castanets look like two really short, fat, shallow wooden spoons tied together with the indented parts facing each other. In order to play them, one castanet is held in the palm of the hand, and the fingers strike the back of the other to clack them together. In orchestral settings, castanets are often mounted for ease of playing. Often used in music with a Spanish influence.
- **Triangle**: Un-pitched. A metal triangle struck with a metal beater.
- **Cymbals**: Un-pitched. Usually two metal concave brass discs struck together for a ringing effect. There are also suspended cymbals, which are single cymbals that can be struck with mallets for various effects. Do an online search for "how cymbals work" to hear the many varieties of sounds that can be created.

Tambourine on the left, castanets on the right; from an engraving by Gustave Doré (1832–1883) titled "Gitana de Grenade dansant le zorongo".

a woman playing the triangle in an etching by Angelica Kauffman (1741–1807) titled "L'Allegra".

- **Gong**: Pitched. Gongs are metal discs of many different sizes struck with mallets.
- **Tam-Tam**: Un-pitched. A tam-tam is a large metal disc struck with a large mallet.
- **Bass drum**: Un-pitched. A large drum, struck with a large mallet. Marching bands usually include a bass drum line with bass drums of various sizes.
- There are many other drums and percussive instruments, including tenor drums, bongos, congas, tom-toms, cowbells, steel-pans, slapsticks, ethnic drums, and household items.

Keyboard Instruments

- **Piano**: The standard keyboard instrument. Many varieties, but mainly upright pianos (used in domestic or classroom settings) and grand pianos (used in professional venues). The sound is created when the performer pushes down the keys on the keyboard. Each key activates a felt-tipped hammer inside the body of the instrument, which in turn strikes a string. (Because of this striking motion, pianos are often classified as percussion instruments.) There are also pedals to either allow the sound to resonate or to muffle the sound. When the piano was first invented, it was called a *pianoforte* because it can play at both the *piano* level of dynamic and the *forte* level of dynamic (and all dynamics in between) depending on how hard the performer strikes the keys.

Piano

Fig. 2.26: Copyright © Steinway & Sons (CC BY-SA 3.0) at https://commons.wikimedia.org/wiki/File:Steinway_%26_Sons_concert_grand_piano,_model_D-274,_manufactured_at_Steinway%27s_factory_in_Hamburg,_Germany.png.

- **Organ**: Seen most often in churches and concert halls, each key on the keyboard is attached by airways to a different-sized pipe. In addition, most organs have multiple keyboards stacked one above the other. The performer also has access to panels on each side of the keyboard covered with little knobs or switches called **stops**. Each stop is connected to a different set of pipes. Sets of pipes vary in shape—round or square, flared or tapered—and materials—different kinds of metal and wood—to create a huge variety of tone colors. By pulling a stop out, the performer opens up the airway to that particular set of pipes. If a performer pulls all the stops out, air is being sent to all the pipes. If you've ever heard the

The Mormon Tabernacle Choir, the Orchestra at Temple Square and the Conference Center organ.

phrase "I'm pulling out all the stops tonight!" you now understand the origin. Performers can pre-assign certain stops to certain keyboards. For instance, the right hand might play on the lowest-positioned keyboard using the brass-sounding sets of pipes while the left hand plays on the next keyboard up with the stops set to the wood pipes for a more flute-like sound. Being trained as an organist is quite different from being trained as a pianist because, in addition to using both hands, organists also use their feet to play another keyboard (pedals) at the base of the organ.

- **Harpsichord**: The predecessor to the piano. Instead of activating felt hammers—like the piano—when a performer strikes the keys of a harpsichord, each key activates a small hook, or plectrum, that plucks the string. This produces a tinny, brittle tone color. If you hear a harpsichord, the composition is most likely from the Baroque Era.
- **Celesta** or celeste: The celesta is a glockenspiel in a case with a piano keyboard. When the performer strikes the keys on the keyboard, mallets strike the glockenspiel. The celesta sounds almost identical to the glockenspiel but has the added advantage of being able to produce as many pitches at a time as there are fingers on the performer.

Sara Scuderi (1906–1987), soprano, best known for her interpretations of the lead role in Puccini's Tosca. Was under contract for many years at Milan's famous opera house, La Scala.

Luciano Pavarotti (1935–2007), one of the most famous tenors of all time.

Voice Types

- **Soprano**: This is the highest female voice. The typical range of a soprano is from middle C (on the piano keyboard) to two octaves above middle C.
- **Mezzo-soprano**: This is the next-highest female voice. The typical range of a mezzo-soprano is an interval of a third below the soprano.
- **Alto**: This is generally the lowest female voice. The typical range of an alto is an interval of a third below the mezzo-soprano.
- **Boy soprano**: Has the same range as soprano but a different tone color. Usually boy sopranos have a more-glassy tone color and use less (if any) vibrato.
- **Countertenor**: A high male voice, approximately the same range as a female alto. The countertenor voice can be a falsetto voice or a true voice, meaning the vocal cords have been carefully trained to sing in that range.
- **Tenor**: The most common high male voice. The typical range is about a fifth below an alto.
- **Baritone**: The middle male voice. Typical range is about a third below a tenor.
- **Bass**: The low male voice. The typical range is about a third below a baritone.

FURTHER INVESTIGATION:

Get to know the sounds of each of the main instruments and voice types used in art music. Work your way through the list above methodically finding recordings or videos online featuring each in an art music setting. A simple keyword search of the name of the instrument or voice type will yield many recordings. For some instruments, such as saxophone, that are better known for their use in jazz or pop music, you may need to modify your keyword search thusly: "classical saxophone." For each instrument, find and listen to as many recordings as you need to ensure that you will recognize the sound of each instrument. (Note: For many instruments, such as the piano, you may already be able to identify its sound without listening to any examples.)

ENSEMBLES OF ART MUSIC

The word **ensemble** generally means group. The following are the main ensembles common in the world of art music.

Instrumental Ensembles

Orchestra
An **orchestra** is a large ensemble that features mostly string instruments. Depending on the time period, the number of woodwind, brass, percussion, and keyboard instruments varies widely. Orchestras are sometimes called **Symphony Orchestra** or **Symphony** for short; they are also sometimes called **Philharmonic** or **Philharmonia**.

Baroque orchestra
In the Baroque Era, the orchestra varied widely in size. Some Baroque orchestral works were composed for as few as seven instrumentalists, while others require over eighty instruments. The standard Baroque orchestra likely had three or four first violins (all playing the same part), three or four 2nd violins, three or four violas, one or two cellos, one double-bass, and one keyboard instrument, most likely harpsichord or organ. Depending on the composer (and possibly the person who commissioned the composition) there may be various woodwind, brass, and percussion instruments. Most common were flutes, oboes, and bassoons (woodwind instruments); trumpet and horn (brass instruments); and timpani (percussion).

Classical orchestra
In the Classical Era, the orchestra became much more standardized in size, and all the different instrument families were represented. Strings: six first violins, six 2nd violins, four violas, two cellos, one or two double-basses. Woodwinds: two flutes, two oboes, two clarinets, two bassoons. Brass: two trumpets, two to four horns (less common, but occasionally trombones and tuba were used). Percussion: timpani and various other bells and cymbals (but used sparingly).

The Simon Bolivar Orchestra (from Venezuela), conducted by Gustavo Dudamel at a concert in Sao Paulo, Brazil in 2013. Dudamel is one of the most sought-after conductors of the present day.

Romantic orchestra

In the Romantic Era, the orchestra grew considerably in size. Strings: at least double the number used in the previous time period. Woodwinds: two flutes, one piccolo; two oboes, one English horn; two clarinets, one bass clarinet; two bassoons, one contrabassoon. (Depending on the composer, sometimes the woodwinds were increased even more, including a new instrument, the saxophone.) Brass: two trumpets; four horns; two tenor trombones, one bass trombone; and tuba. (Again, depending on composer, sometimes the brass were increased even more.) Percussion: timpani, snare drum, bass drum, gong, cymbals of all varieties, castanets, triangle, chimes, xylophone.

Twentieth-Century orchestra and Contemporary orchestra

From the Twentieth Century onward, the basic Romantic orchestra is the standard. In addition, various composers introduce new instruments whenever it suits their purposes—truly anything goes. Electronic instruments, car horns, and manipulated recordings are all fair game in modern music.

Pit orchestra

A pit orchestra is used in the art music genres of opera and ballet. It is located in a pit in front of (and lower than) the stage or partially underneath the stage. Pit orchestras vary in size and instrumentation depending on the time period.

Wind ensemble

Also referred to as **wind symphony**, **concert band**, and **symphonic band**, wind ensembles feature woodwind, brass, and percussion instruments. Because there are no strings involved (except for a lone double-bass or harp on occasion), all the woodwind and brass instruments are in greater numbers than you would find in an orchestra. For example, instead of the two or three clarinets you would find in a typical orchestra, there could be up to twenty in a wind ensemble. Wind ensembles often play transcriptions or arrangements of orchestral repertoire, but there is an increasing number of compositions composed specifically for the wind ensemble.

Chamber music

Chamber music refers to ensembles of a smaller size than an orchestra, usually a group of between two and twenty performers. Numerous combinations are possible—duo, trio, quartet, quintet, sextet, septet, octet, nonet, dectet, hendectet, and more. Among the most common are

- **Piano Trio** (usually violin, cello, piano)
- **String Quartet** (usually two violins, one viola, one cello)
- **Piano Quintet** (string quartet and piano)
- **Wind Quintet** (flute, oboe, clarinet, bassoon, horn)
- **Brass Quintet** (two trumpets, trombone, horn, tuba)

Chamber music is so called because, originally, music written for these smaller ensembles was intended to be performed in someone's chamber, or, in other words, in his/her living room. Louis XIV, for instance, would have court musicians perform not only in his living-room chamber but in his bed chamber to wake him in the morning, in his dining chamber while he ate meals, and, disturbingly, in his bath chamber.

Vocal Ensembles

- **Chorus** is a vocal ensemble that generally specializes in secular music.
- **Choir** is a vocal ensemble that generally specializes in sacred music.

CHAPTER THREE
Attending Concerts

Concert Etiquette

Attending a professional musical performance should always be a fun and fulfilling experience. It can also be a daunting or disorienting experience if you are unaware of the generally accepted concert etiquette. This is similar to attending a sporting event for the first time. As soon as the attendee becomes aware of expected behavioral norms, the experience is much more enjoyable.

Arriving:
Do everything in your power to arrive on time. If you are late, do not walk to your seat during a piece of music. Wait until you hear applause; you may then enter without interrupting the actual performance. At some venues, you may enter between movements of a particular piece. But whatever you do, once you're in the hall, do everything in your power to get to your seat swiftly and quietly. Do not be a distraction to the rest of the audience.

Leaving:
Do not leave during a piece of music. Wait until there is applause; you may then leave without interrupting the actual performance. Exceptions to this include uncontrollable coughing or if you are having a medical emergency—in those cases, please leave as swiftly as possible to ensure your health.

Behavior:
During a musical performance, you should not make any noise. Keep in mind that music performances are truly the live creation of art. Making noise during

a musical performance is akin to wiping your hand across the wet canvas of a professional painter. Here are just *some* of the noises that could disturb people sitting near you:

- Opening crinkly candy wrappers: If you must have candy or a cough drop, wait to unwrap it until there is applause.
- Talking: Even if you think you can whisper really softly, everyone in the room— including the performers on stage—can still hear your "esses."
- Coughing/Sneezing: If you need to cough, do everything in your power to hold it in until the end of the piece or movement. Sneezes sometimes catch you off guard, but if you feel one coming on, pinch the bridge of your nose or press against your top lip. And if all else fails and you *have* to sneeze or cough, shove your face as firmly into your inner elbow as possible to muffle the noise.
- Clicking pens: Many people have a habit of clicking their pens without even realizing that they are doing it. Don't be that person.
- Using electronic devices: It is inappropriate to use electronic devices. The light from the device distracts those sitting behind you. Plus, no matter how softly you think you can type on a keyboard, the little clicks can still be heard throughout the hall.
- Cellphones: Turn your cellphones completely off. Cell phone signals can interfere with recording devices.
- Tapping feet: It's noisy. Don't do it.
- Fidgeting of young children: If you bring young children with you, keep them silent throughout the performance. In general, it is considered inappropriate to bring children younger than six years old, and, depending on the maturity level of the child, perhaps not even younger than twelve years old. Some performance venues have minimum age requirements.

When is it appropriate to clap?

You can clap at the end of a piece of music. Do not clap after a single movement of a multi-movement work—wait until all the movements have occurred before clapping. And please wait until the piece of music is truly *over* before clapping. There are occasionally people in the audience who desire so badly to be the first person to clap that they start clapping during the final note of a piece. If the conductor's arms are still up, or if the performers instruments are still in playing position, don't clap. Exceptions: When attending a ballet, you may clap *during* the music if the dancer(s) did something particularly praiseworthy. When attending an opera, you may clap after arias or choruses, and at the end of each scene or act.

When is it appropriate to yell things?

There are only certain things you should yell at a music performance, and *only* during applause.

- You may yell *encore* if you want the performers to perform again.
- You may yell *bravo* if you loved the performance and clapping isn't expressive enough. (If you want to be technically correct, yell *bravo* if the performer is a man, *brava* if the performer is a woman, and *bravi* if you are cheering for multiple performers.)
- Even the "woo!" sound, once reserved for less formal occasions, is becoming increasingly common (and perfectly acceptable) in art-music venues.
- You may even yell "boo" if you truly thought the performance was atrocious, but be prepared for angry looks from people sitting near you.

When is it appropriate to give a standing ovation?

Give a standing ovation only when you were swept away by the music to such an extent that mere clapping is not enough to show your joy. Standing ovations are also a nice way to show that you would like to hear an encore number.

How to dress:

This depends entirely on the venue. If you are paying to see a professional ensemble perform, dress up. If you are attending a performance on a college campus, and you don't have time to go home between your last class and the performance, go as you are. Performers would rather have you there than not. You will see people dressed formally and informally at practically every venue. On opening night at the ballet or the opera, or the start of an orchestra's season, you will see people dressed in full tuxedos and evening gowns, as well as a few people in jeans and a t-shirt.

Things to Look for at a Performance

Obtain a program and read it:

Programs contain lots of helpful information and can actually make your experience much more exciting. The essential elements listed in the program can help you understand what you are about to hear. For instance, as you learn more about the genres, styles, and forms of the different time periods, you will recognize certain terms as part of titles. Then, when you read a title of a piece listed in the program, you will have at least a small idea of what you're about to hear. Next to each title, you will find the name of the composer and his/her birth (and death) date. This helps you pinpoint the time period in which the piece was written. As you learn about historical compositional characteristics, even a birth date can help you know something about what you are about to hear. Some performing-arts organizations will even include program notes in the printed program. Program notes are detailed descriptions of the pieces you are going to hear.

Watch the performers/conductor:

You can gain a lot from attending a music performance simply by watching the performers exhibit their emotions and passion as they perform. Singers, particularly, are very expressive both with facial expressions and physical movement in their efforts to share the emotion or the storyline of the piece they are performing. When pianists or other instrumentalists make huge physical gestures during a performance, they are not merely posturing or acting; in most cases, they are unaware of their physicality—they are simply allowing the music to move them as they perform.

Meet the performers:

Depending on the venue, it may or may not be appropriate to go backstage to talk to the performers, but if you have the opportunity, take advantage of it. Performers appreciate hearing how the music moved you. They want to know that what they are doing is of value to the listeners.

MIDDLE AGES (450-1450)

The majority of written music preserved from the Middle Ages is sacred. The clergy were educated and literate; as a result, they were able to write the music down so future listeners could enjoy it. In addition, the way music was performed in the Catholic Church lent itself to preservation because it was passed down from generation to generation.

Instruments in the Middle Ages

None of the instruments common today existed in the Middle Ages. There are earlier versions of flutes, recorders, violins, guitars, trombones, and percussion, but they are not called by those names. For instance, the medieval trombone is called a *sackbut*.

Performance Venues in the Middle Ages

Many of the performance venues common today did not exist in the Middle Ages. For instance, there was no such thing as a concert hall, recital hall or opera house. The two most important performance venues in the Middle Ages are the church and the court. The church is an important performance venue due to the large amount of music used in church services such as the Mass. Music is also performed in homes. In the homes of the nobility, music is performed by court musicians and by the nobility themselves. In the homes of the lower classes, music is performed wherever the skill and inclination exist.

CHAPTER FOUR

Compositional and Performance Techniques of the Middle Ages

Performance Technique: A cappella Singing

A cappella describes singing that is not accompanied by musical instruments. The term literally means "to the chapel" or "in the style of the chapel," because early church music was sung without instrumental accompaniment.

Genres that feature a cappella singing:
- Mass
- Motets
- Organa
- Plainchant

Compositional Technique: Church Modes

A **mode** is a scale. Before the development of the major/minor scale system that we use today, there were a number of modes that were used in the Middle Ages. They each sound somewhat similar to the major/minor scale system, but the order of half steps and whole steps is different enough to make

Singing a *cappella* in the Middle Ages. Before the advent of printing presses, church choirs would have to gather around a single, large hand-written book of music.

them sound somewhat foreign to us. It was believed, at the time, that the modes could influence the way the listener felt and/or behaved. As a result, the Catholic Church approved only certain modes for use in the church. It felt that certain modes were more likely to turn the listener's minds toward heaven and other modes were more likely to lead to sin. This may strike a modern person as simplistic or silly, but in reality, most of us would readily agree that we listen to certain kinds of music when in a good mood and other kinds of music when in a bad mood.

Musician Angels and the Harrowing of Hell; detail from an illuminated manuscript (1290).

Angel with a drone.

Genres that use church modes:

All the sacred genres in the Middle Ages (and part of the Renaissance) used these modes.

Are church modes used in music composed after the Middle Ages?

Modes were used throughout the Middle Ages and much of the Renaissance, but hardly at all beyond that. Nowadays, modes are occasionally used by composers who are striving to achieve a certain sound. Modes are also used in jazz music.

Performance Technique: Drone

A **drone** is a sustained, continuous pitch. Drones can be produced by a string instrument, a wind instrument, or a very basic tabletop organ (organs in the Middle Ages are simple keyboards—not at all like the keyboards of today—with one pipe per key and a small bellows to provide air for the pipes). Drones are still used in music today in period ensembles, bagpipe music, and some contemporary compositions.

Genres that use a drone:

Plainchant occasionally featured the use of drones starting sometime in the middle of the Middle Ages. This was instituted by the performers, not the composers, hence a plainchant using a drone is still considered a plainchant despite the shift from monophony to homophony. Many secular genres in the Middle Ages also use drones.

Compositional Technique: Isorhythm

Isorhythm is a very specific type of recurring rhythm used in the latter half of the Middle Ages. It is usually located in the lowest sung line of medieval motets. Although the rhythm repeats, the note patterns do not; same rhythm, different melody. As a result, it takes a skilled and discerning ear to actually be aware of the presence of isorhythm. It is helpful to have the printed music in front of you to see it visually.

Genres that use isorhythm:
Numerous, but most often found in medieval motets.

Is isorhythm used in music composed after the Middle Ages?
Not really. Occasionally, later composers (particularly in the Twentieth Century) use isorhythm, but not to the same extent as it was used in the Middle Ages.

See the following page for an example of isorhythm.

4

PHILIPP DE VITRY

Hugo princeps - Cum structura

Dm. d. Tk. in Oest. XL 76

Example of isorhythm. Look at the "I1" indication, then the "I2" indication. Note that the rhythm of I1 in the bass line is repeated perfectly at I2. The pitches change, but the rhythm stays the same. Then notice the rhythm in the top line at I1 and notice how it repeats at I2. Isorhythm is easy to see on a score like this, but very difficult to hear because it has nothing to do with the notes and everything to do with the rhythm.

CHAPTER FIVE
Genres of the Middle Ages

Mass

In the Catholic Church there are many possible church services each day. Arguably, the most important of these is the **Mass**.

The Mass, and what determines the text/music used each day, is fairly complex, but the basic components are as follows:

Certain texts within the Mass change from day to day; these are known as **Proper** texts. Throughout the year, the church calendar is filled with holidays unique to Christendom and feast days. Feast days are usually associated with particular saints or events in the life of Christ. On such days, the texts known as Proper would be scriptures/liturgical writings about that particular saint or event. There are also Masses for other purposes such as funerary rites; these Masses are known as Requiem Masses.

There are other texts that are the same every time you attend Mass; these are known as **Ordinary** texts. The five sections of the Mass in which the texts stay the same, and thus labeled Ordinary, are 1) **Kyrie**, 2) **Gloria**, 3) **Credo**, 4) **Sanctus**, and 5) **Agnus Dei**.

Historically, composers spent more time and effort on creating elaborate music for the Ordinary sections of the Mass, whereas the Proper sections were simpler. For instance, in the Middle Ages, the Proper sections featured simple recitation (see *plainchant*) and the Ordinary sections featured much more intricate music, perhaps with larger intervals, and maybe even polyphony. The composers did this because the text used for the Proper was used only on that specific day each year (if at all), whereas the text for the Ordinary was used daily. Composers, therefore, hoping for their music to be heard more frequently, leaned toward setting the texts that were heard more

Depiction of a Mass; from an illuminated manuscript.

frequently. The Mass continues to be a vital part of the Catholic Church service, and, therefore, is a vital music genre.

Performing forces for Masses:

A cappella voices were the most common performing forces in the Middle Ages. At some point, drones were introduced, possibly to help the singers stay on pitch with more ease.

Does the genre of Mass exist beyond the Middle Ages?

Yes. The genre of Mass continues to be a viable music genre to the present day. Masses (or sections from Masses) from the Middle Ages are still performed regularly in churches around the world. Masses were composed in subsequent time periods as well, right up to the present day. Throughout history the text of the Mass has stayed relatively the same, but the musical style has changed from time period to time period. If you hear a Mass composed in the Renaissance, it will sound considerably different from a Mass composed in the Middle Ages.

FURTHER INVESTIGATION:

1. Attend a Catholic Mass. If available, obtain a printed program so you can look for the Ordinary sections of the Mass. Notice the texture of the different sections of the Mass to see if the Ordinary sections are more elaborate than the Proper sections. It is likely that masses you attend will have a variety of music from different time periods.
2. Watch or listen to a Mass composed in the Middle Ages. Notice the texture of the different sections of the Mass to see if the Ordinary sections are more elaborate than the Proper sections.

SUGGESTED LISTENING:

Any music from a Middle Ages Mass. Search online for keywords "Gregorian chant," "Codex Sanblasianus," or "Liber Usualis."

Plainchant

Plainchant—also known as Gregorian chant, plainsong, or, simply, chant—is the main type of music heard in the Catholic Church for the first half of the Middle Ages. Most of the music in the Mass and the other daily church services was plainchant. The main characteristics of chant are

- Monophonic: No harmony
- Non-metrical: No regular sense of pulse
- Modal: Composed using church modes
- Latin text: There is one Ordinary text in the Mass—the Kyrie—which is in Greek, but the rest of the Mass is in Latin. Note: In the mid-1960s the Catholic Church changed policy and allowed the High Mass to be sung in the language of the country in which it was performed.

Plainchant flourished from the beginning of the Middle Ages through about the year 900 when polyphonic compositions began to evolve.

Performing forces for plainchant:

A cappella voices.

Compositional techniques used in plainchant:

- **Syllabic** text settings: Contain one note per syllable

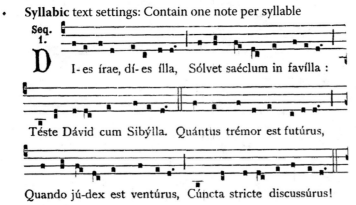

Mostly syllabic text setting in a plainchant excerpt from the *Dies Irae* section of the Requiem Mass.

- **Neumatic** text settings: Contain a few notes per syllable
- **Melismatic** text settings: Contain a lot of notes per syllable

Neumatic text setting.
Copyright in the Public Domain.

Melismatic text setting on the syllables "me" and "cle."
Copyright © G. Rosa-Grosasm (CC BY-SA 4.0) at https://commons.wikimedia.org/wiki/File:Tropo_melisma_musical_in_medio_ecclesiae.png.

General types of plainchant:

There are many different kinds of plainchant. The main types are

- **Recitation:** Chant in which one pitch is dominant throughout with only small deviations from the pitch at the beginning of the phrase or at the cadence. These chants can be quite monotonous but can also be hypnotic and calming.

An example of recitation; note the pitch that seems to repeat almost constantly.
Copyright in the Public Domain

- **Responsory:** Chant in which there is a call and response effect; one singer sings a phrase of music, then a group of singers sings a phrase of music, then back to the solo singer, back to the group, and so on.
- **Non-responsory:** Chants in which there is no call and response effect.

Other types of chant you might see in a printed program at a Mass service (with its definition):

- Alleluia: Melismatic responsorial plainchant
- Antiphon: Responsorial plainchant with melismas used at the cadences or occasionally to embellish a word or phrase
- Gradual: Highly melismatic plainchant
- Introit: The first thing you'll hear at a Mass, the introductory antiphon
- Sequence: Syllabic plainchants (with small neumatic moments) with an AA BB CC DD, etc., form
- Tract: Non-responsorial, mainly neumatic and syllabic plainchant, with melismas at the cadences
- Trope: A technique by which extra liturgical phrases are added to other texts. If an Ordinary section has had tropes added, it is no longer Ordinary, it is Proper.

About halfway through the Middle Ages, performers started adding a drone to their performances of plainchant.

Does the genre of plainchant exist beyond the Middle Ages?

Yes, somewhat. Even up to the present day, plainchants from the Middle Ages are still performed in church services. In general, composers after the Middle Ages did not compose new plainchants. Other genres captured their interest.

FURTHER INVESTIGATION:

1. Attend a Catholic Church service. Try to find a Catholic Church that has a good choir. Pay attention to how much recitation you hear versus neumatic or melismatic chants. After the Middle Ages, when homophonic music was the norm, resourceful composers wrote organ accompaniment or other harmonies to the original plainchants, so you may hear a blend of new and old when you attend a church service.

2. Pick a chant from the list above (for example, "Antiphon" or "Introit") and listen to or watch five or six of them online to see if you can identify their chief characteristics.

3. Search online for the *Liber Usualis* (a collection of chants following the church calendar). Near the start of the *Liber Usualis*, there are illustrated instructions on how to read the older style of writing music. Using your newfound knowledge, try to sing a few of the chants found therein.

SUGGESTED LISTENING:

- Anonymous: Since most church composers chose to remain anonymous (to give the glory to God), do a keyword search for chant or plainchant or Gregorian chant or *Liber Usualis*.
- Hildegard von Bingen's *Ordo virtutum*
- Notker Balbulus' *Gaude Maria virgo*

Organa/Organum

Around the middle of the Middle Ages (900), an interesting development took place in church music—the addition of polyphonic compositions to the church service. These compositions are called **organa** (**organum** in the singular). To compose an organum, composers take a preexisting chant and write a new melodic line to be sung at the same time as the preexisting chant. This second melody can be written either above or below the chant. Both voice parts sing the same syllables at the same time. The development of organa went through a number of stages.

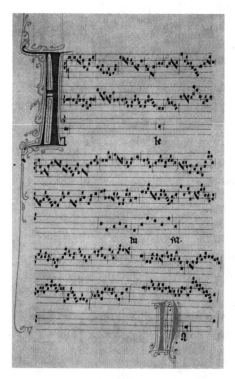

Organum Triplum by Perotin.

Stage one:
At first, organa were composed in parallel motion. In other words, if the notes in the preexisting chant were ascending or descending, the notes in the new melody did the same.

Stage two:
As composers became accustomed to this early polyphony, they began composing in a blend of parallel motion and contrary motion.

An organum in which the preexisting chant is joined by one new melody is called an organum duplum.

Stage three:
As composers continued exploring this new genre, they started to set one voice melismatically and one voice syllabically; each voice still sings the same syllables at the same time.

Stage four:

After a while, composers started adding *more* than one new melody to create an organum triplum or organum quadruplum. They could add as many new melodies to the original chant as they want, but, again, all the voices sing the same syllables at the same time.

Stage five:

Eventually, composers relegated the original chant to the lowest part and sustained each note for a long time—almost like a drone. The new voices, on the other hand, are full of melismas. The compositional interest is most certainly located in the new voices, not the preexisting chant.

Performing forces for organa:

A cappella voices. When the original chant was stretched out into really long notes, sometimes the human voice would be replaced by a drone. But in general, organa are performed *a cappella*.

Does the genre of organa exist beyond the Middle Ages?

Yes, but only insofar as the organa composed in the Middle Ages are still performed as part of church services. Composers after the Middle Ages did not compose new organa.

FURTHER INVESTIGATION:

Search online for "organum" and listen to five different organa (audio or video). Try to determine at what stage each example is in the development of organa.

SUGGESTED LISTENING:

- Léonin's *Notum feci Dominus salutare suum ante conspectum gentium revelavit justitiam suam* (organum duplum)
- Perotin's *Alleluia Nativitas* (organum triplum)
- Perotin's *Viderunt omnes fines terre salutare dei nostri jubilate deo omnis terra* (organum quadruplum)

Troubadour Songs

Most of the written music we have from the Middle Ages was written down by educated members of the clergy. We don't have much secular music because most of the secular composers were illiterate; they couldn't write it down to preserve it.

A troubadour performing; from a collection of troubadour songs from the mid-1200's.

The secular music that we *do* have was composed by people who could afford an education. The types of people who fall into this category are 1) members of the nobility and 2) educated musicians who worked in the homes of the wealthy as their personal, in-house composers. Music was a common hobby among the nobility and many were trained in the art of music performance and composition. These composers are referred to as **troubadours, trobairitz, trouvères,** and **Minnesingers**, depending on the region of Europe in which they lived. For ease of explanation, the catch-all term *troubadour* will be used. Note: Troubadours are not the same as wandering minstrels; troubadours stay put, whereas minstrels wander from town to town.

The subject matter of **troubadour songs** is most often secular: drinking songs, songs about glorious battles or knights saving princesses, and the most popular topic of secular songs—love and/or lust. In fact, it is sometimes surprising for modern ears to hear the words to certain secular songs from the Middle Ages and realize how ribald they are.

Performing forces for troubadour songs:

Performing forces depend on 1) the composer's personal preferences, 2) which instruments are available, and 3) who the singer is. But a good generalization is a solo singer. Often, there may have been some string or wind accompaniment (or maybe both) and occasionally a basic drum to provide some rhythm. But unlike the fully formed chords used in modern secular music as a harmonic support to the melody, the accompaniment to troubadour songs is often one or two notes played in an alternating rhythmic pattern. Also, depending on the performer, a solo instrument might play the melody at the same time as the singer.

Types of troubadour songs:

This is only a small sampling of the many sub-genres within the genre of troubadour songs.

- Alba: Song about two lovers parting as the sun rises, often warned by a friend standing guard of the approach of one or both of their spouses
- Escondig: Song in which a man apologizes to a lady for his inappropriate behavior.
- Gab: A bragging song

- Pastorela: Song about a knight encountering a shepherd girl and the results of such a meeting; could be bawdy or comical in nature
- Planh: Song mourning the death of royalty
- Salut d'amour: A love letter song

Does the genre of troubadour songs exist beyond the Middle Ages?

Yes. You can still hear troubadour songs from the Middle Ages performed regularly by both professional and amateur period ensembles at formal concerts, Medieval (and Renaissance) fairs, Shakespearean festivals, and similar events throughout the world. There are radio and online programs that exclusively feature music of the Middle Ages. Films set in the Middle Ages, or even in a fantasy world that resembles the Middle Ages (like *Lord of the Rings*), often use actual troubadour songs or have songs within the film that are inspired by—or that try to mimic—the sound of troubadour songs. In general, composers after the Middle Ages do not compose troubadour songs.

Exceptions to the definition above:

The vast majority of troubadour songs are secular in nature, but there are some troubadour songs with religious subject matter. These particular songs deal with efforts to avoid sin and to express the joy of repentance and the goodness of God. Despite the sacred subject matter, these were not performed in church.

FURTHER INVESTIGATION:

Search online for any of the sub-genres of troubadour songs listed above and listen to them taking note of which characteristics they manifest.

SUGGESTED LISTENING:

- Bernart de Ventadorn's *Lanquan vei la folha*
- Bernger von Horheim's *Nu enbeiz ich doch des trankes nie*
- Moniot d'Arras' *Ce fut en mai*

Motet

The **motet** in the Middle Ages is composed in almost exactly the same manner as an organum; in other words, composers begin by selecting a preexisting plainchant, then add to it one or more new melodic lines. Unlike organa, each vocal line has its own unique text. The motet began as a sacred genre, with each added melody line featuring either liturgical text or a poem about a sacred matter.

This compositional technique created a unique challenge to the listener, namely that of comprehension. When two or three vocal lines occur at the same time with two or three separate texts, it can become quite cluttered-sounding.

At some point in the Middle Ages, composers began using non-sacred texts for the additional melody lines, which made the motet even more unusual—multiple texts, some sacred, some secular, all overlapping at the same time.

As a result of the use of multiple texts, the way motets are titled is unique in music history. The first few words of each text are included in the title, separated by slashes or dashes like so:

O nobilis nativitas—O mira dei—O decus virgineum—Apparuit

or

Salve mater redemptoris/Salve lux langentium/Salve sine spina

Performing forces for motets:

Most often, motets are performed *a cappella*. Occasionally, the line that features the original plainchant is performed by an instrument (for the same reason as in organa).

Does the genre of motet exist beyond the Middle Ages?

Yes, but with some fairly radical changes. Motets from the Middle Ages are still performed in concerts, on certain radio programs, etc. However, the compositional process of writing a motet was abandoned in the Renaissance, even though the genre of motet still existed. In the Renaissance, motets are composed in a very different manner and, therefore, sound completely different from motets of the Middle Ages.

FURTHER INVESTIGATION:

1. Look at a score of a motet from the Middle Ages. Take note of the multiple texts used (one text per vocal line). If the translations of the text are provided, see if you can determine which texts are sacred and which, if any, are secular. Look at the bottom line to see if you can find an example of isorhythm.

2. Listen to motets (make sure they're from the Middle Ages) to take note of how cluttered the multiple texts can sound and to see if you can hear the isorhythm. Remember, isorhythm is usually quite difficult to hear because it is often located in the lowest voice part—not one of the melodies. This would be most effective if you have the score in hand so you can follow along as you listen.

SUGGESTED LISTENING:

- Guillaume de Machaut's *Fias volontas tua/Qui plus aimme/Aucune gent*
- John Dunstable's *Gaude virgo salutata/Gaude virgo singularis/Virgo mater comprobaris/Ave gemma, JD 28*
- Philippe de Vitry's *Trahunt in precipicia/Quasi non ministerium/Ve qui gregi*

CHAPTER

SIX

Composers of
the Middle Ages

Anonymous

Many composers of the Middle Ages chose to remain anonymous. In sacred music, this may have been because church composers were members of holy orders (monks and nuns) composing music with the express purpose of glorifying God; to avoid the sin of pride, they remained anonymous. In secular genres, most composers attached their names to their compositions, but some, who were members of the nobility, felt that composing was a lowly profession and didn't want to be seen doing something below their station. This resulted in a number of secular pieces written by "Anonymous."

Arras, Moniot d' (c. 1200–1240)

Country: France
Known for: Trouvère songs
Recommended listening: *Ce fut en mai*

Dunstable, John (c. 1385–1450)

Country: England
Known for: Masses
Recommended listening: *Agnus Dei, JD 14*

Hildegard receiving inspiration from heaven; detail from the Ruperts-berger Codex (mid 1100's).

Francesco Landini playing a portative organ (a drone); tomb in Basilica di San Lorenzo, Florence, Italy.

Halle, Adam de la (c. 1235–1285)

<u>Country:</u> France
<u>Known for:</u> Trouvère songs
<u>Recommended listening:</u> Le jeu de Robin et de Marion

Hildegard of Bingen (1098–1179)

- She was the tenth child of her parents, and was subsequently *tithed* to the church when she was a young girl (sources vary on age—anywhere from eight to fourteen)[1] and became a nun.
- She had visions throughout her life, including as a young child. Wrote a number of books on a wide range of topics including science, medicine, religion, and her visions.[2]
- She has been referred to as a saint for a very long time, but her sainthood was made official only quite recently—by Pope Benedict XVI in October of 2012.[3]

<u>Country:</u> Germany
<u>Known for:</u> Plainchant
<u>Recommended listening:</u> *Ordo Virtutum (Play of the Virtues)*—a liturgical drama about the struggle for the human soul between the devil and the virtues.

Landini, Francesco (c. 1325–1395)

- As a child, he went blind due to smallpox.
- Despite his blindness, he was an organ builder, instrument maker, poet, and composer.

<u>Country:</u> Italy
<u>Known for:</u> Ballatas (a type of song)
<u>Recommended listening:</u> *Deh, dimmi tu*

---

1   Fiona Maddocks, *Hildegard of Bingen: The Woman of Her Age* (New York: Doubleday, 2001), 17–18.
2   Fiona Bowie and Oliver Davies, eds. *Hildegard of Bingen: Mystical Writings* (New York: Crossroad, 1993), 10–13.
3   "Apostolic Letter Proclaiming Saint Hildegard of Bingen, professed nun of the Order of Saint Benedict, a Doctor of the Universal Church," Vatican website, accessed June 16, 2016, http://w2.vatican.va/content/benedict-xvi/en/apost_letters/documents/hf_ben-xvi_apl_20121007_ildegarda-bingen.html.

Léonin (c. 1150-1200)

<u>Country:</u> France
<u>Known for:</u> Organa
<u>Recommended listening:</u> *Propter Veritatem*

Einzug des Minnesängers Ulrich von Liechtenstein.

Ulrich von Liechtenstein (on horseback).

Liechtenstein, Ulrich von (c. 1200-1275)

- In the 2001 film *A Knight's Tale*, one of the main characters, played by actor Heath Ledger, takes a false name in an attempt to appear as a member of the nobility. The name he uses is "Ulrich von Liechtenstein." Sadly, the film makes no connection to Liechtenstein's abilities as a composer.[4]
- Even though we have the lyrics and many references to the quality of his songs, none of the music has survived.[5]

Ulrich von Liechtenstein (statue in Graz, Austria).

---

4 "A Knight's Tale," Wikipedia.org, accessed June 16, 2016, https://en.wikipedia.org/wiki/A_Knight%27s_Tale.

5 James V. McMahon, *The Music of Early Minnesang* (Columbia: Camden House, 1990), 76–80.

Country: Austria
Known for: Minnesang (similar to troubadour songs)

Machaut, Guillaume de (c. 1300-1377)

Country: France
Known for: Motets
Recommended listening: *Vidi Dominum/Faus Samblant/Amours qui ha le povoir*

Perotin (c. 1160-c. 1215)

Country: France
Known for: Organa
Recommended listening: *Alleluia Nativitas*

Ventadorn, Bernart de (c. 1135-c. 1195)

Country: France
Known for: Troubadour songs
Recommended listening: *Amors, e que-us es vejaire*

Vitry, Philippe de (1291-1361)

Country: France
Known for: Motets
Recommended listening: *Aman novi/Heu Fortuna/Heu me, tristis est anima mea*

Vogelweide, Walther von der (c. 1170-c. 1230)

Country: Germany
Known for: Minnesang
Recommended listening: *Under der linden an der heide*

Wolkenstein, Oswald von (c. 1375-1445)

Country: Germany
Known for: Minnesang
Recommended listening: *Der Mai mit lieber zal*

SECTION 3

RENAISSANCE ERA (1400-1600)

The Renaissance Era is a time of increased educational opportunities for the general public. The development of the printing press enables music to be purchased by the average citizen and distributed much more easily. The rise of the university brings education to more people than ever before. Music in the Renaissance is influenced by the popularity of polyphonic writing for the human voice. Almost every piece of music in the Renaissance features polyphony. In addition, most vocal music in the Renaissance is *a cappella*.

Instruments in the Renaissance

In the Renaissance, earlier versions of the flute, recorder, violin, guitar, and various brass instruments exist, most of which are called by different names.

Performance Venues in the Renaissance

The church and the court continue to be important performance venues during the Renaissance. The home also continues to be an important venue for domestic music genres such as madrigals.

CHAPTER

SEVEN

Compositional and Performance Techniques of the Renaissance

Performance Technique: *A cappella* singing

A cappella singing continued to be popular in the Renaissance.

Genres that feature *a cappella* singing:
- Mass
- Motets
- Madrigals

Compositional Technique: High Renaissance Style

In the **High Renaissance style,** the textures used in any particular piece of music alternate between polyphony (mainly imitative) and homophony. It was as though the composers wanted to show off their abilities to write elaborate polyphony, yet also wanted to show that they could write a lush rich homophony. This style flourished from the middle of the Renaissance right through the end of the era.

Angels singing *a cappella*; detail from the Ghent Altarpiece (early 1400's).

Genres that use the High Renaissance style:
Almost every genre in the second half of the Renaissance uses this style.

Is the High Renaissance style used in music composed after the Renaissance?
No. This style is supplanted by new styles in the Baroque Era.

Compositional Technique: Paraphrase

Renaissance **paraphrase technique** is a technique by which a composer starts with a preexisting melody (usually plainchant) and rewrites it to use within a new composition. Composers can add meter, change the rhythm, add extra notes—in some cases, a lot of extra notes—anything at all to make the melody sound more interesting than its original form. It made sense for Renaissance composers to use plainchants as the basis for a new composition because composers in the previous time period had done the same thing although in different genres (organa, motets). Paraphrase is used quite frequently in Renaissance Masses. After selecting the preexisting chant, composers paraphrase and use it in each Ordinary section of the Mass. This creates a sense of unity throughout the Mass. Even though plainchants are the main type of melody paraphrased, after a time, composers started paraphrasing secular tunes.

Genres that use paraphrase:
• Mass
• Motet

Is paraphrase technique used in music composed after the Renaissance?
Not in the same way. Paraphrases in the Renaissance are based on plainchant and are used in mostly sacred genres. Paraphrases in later time periods are created in substantially different ways.

Compositional Technique: Word Painting

Word painting is a technique by which composers attempt to illustrate, through music, the words being sung. In other words, if the words of a song are "ascending into heav'n," the composer sets that text to an ascending note pattern. Here are some visual examples of word painting:

crick - ets hop and hop and hop and hop and hop and hop and stop.

As you can see, the "hopping" of the words is replicated/illustrated by the written notes. This example would be easily seen and easily heard.

The ser-pent sli - thered all a - round, it sli - thered, sli - thered

In this example, it may not be quite as easy to *hear* the word painting, but, visually, the noteheads appear to outline the shape of a slithering snake.

Word painting continued to be popular in the next time period, although not quite as obviously.

Genres that use word painting:

You can find this technique in practically any Renaissance vocal genre, although it was most used in madrigals. Because madrigals are mainly a domestic genre, a lot of the word-painting is visual in nature—intended more for the entertainment of the singers themselves rather than the audience.

Is word-painting used in music composed after the Renaissance?

Yes. In the Baroque Era it is used in much the same way as in the Renaissance, although in different genres.

CHAPTER
EIGHT
Genres of the Renaissance

Madrigal

A **madrigal** is a song composed using the High Renaissance style (alternating sections of polyphony and homophony) for *a cappella* multiple voices. Madrigals can be either sacred or secular, but the vast majority are secular, with widely varying topics. Initially, madrigals flourished in Italy then spread to other European countries. Madrigals often feature word painting, sometimes to an extreme degree. Madrigals from England are particularly popular to this day.

Performing forces for madrigals:
A cappella singers.

Compositional techniques used in madrigals:
- High Renaissance style
- Word painting

Does the genre of the madrigal exist beyond the Renaissance?
Yes, but only insofar as they are still performed to the present day. Many professional vocal ensembles specialize in the performance of madrigals. The composition of new madrigals is highly infrequent (if not entirely absent) after the end of the Renaissance.

One vocal part from a madrigal; from a collection of madrigals published in 1589.

FURTHER INVESTIGATION:

1. Listen to a number of madrigals (composed in the Renaissance) to see if you can hear the word painting and the use of the High Renaissance style.
2. Look at the text of an English madrigal before you listen to it to see if you can determine which words will be "painted." Then listen to it to see if you were right.
3. Listen to an Italian madrigal without the text in front of you and try to guess which words are being painted simply by listening. Then look at a translation of the text to see if you are correct.

SUGGESTED LISTENING:

- Luca Marenzio's *Solo e pensoso i piu deserti campi*
- Carlo Gesualdo's *Moro, lasso, al mio duolo*
- Michael East's *Quick, quick, away, dispatch!*
- John Farmer's *Fair Phyllis I Saw Sitting All Alone* and *A Little Pretty Bonny Lass*

Motet

Renaissance motets are quite different from the motets of the Middle Ages. Renaissance motets are sacred *a cappella* vocal music composed using the High

Renaissance style. In many ways they are almost exactly like madrigals except for the fact that they are sacred in nature (mostly) and the text is in Latin.

Performing forces for motets:

A cappella voices.

Compositional techniques used in Renaissance motets:

- High Renaissance style
- Word painting

Does the genre of the motet exist beyond the Renaissance? Yes, somewhat. Renaissance motets are still performed today. There are many professional vocal ensembles that specialize in the performance of Renaissance vocal music. Motets continue to be composed in subsequent time periods, but they use different compositional methods and styles and therefore sound quite different from motets of the Renaissance.

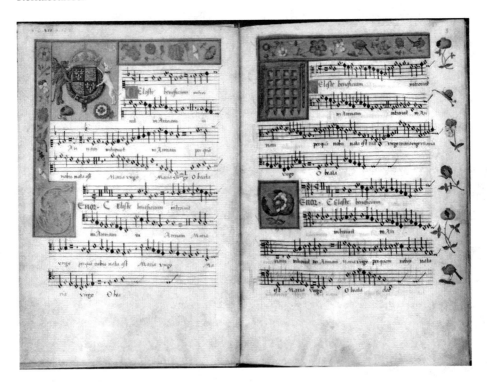

A four part motet—*Celeste beneficium*, by Jean Mouton; from a book of motets created for King Henry VIII of England in the early 1500's.

FURTHER INVESTIGATION:

1. Listen to a number of motets (composed in the Renaissance) to see if you can hear the use of the High Renaissance style.
2. Listen to a few Renaissance motets and then listen to a few motets from the Middle Ages. Note the differences.

SUGGESTED LISTENING:

- Jan Pieterszoon Sweelinck's *Hodie Christus natus est*
- Orlando de Lasso's *Quare tristis es anima mea?*
- William Byrd's *Domine, tu jurasti*

Mass

The structural and textual elements of the Mass in the Renaissance are the same as in the Middle Ages. The main difference is in the compositional techniques used. Plainchants and *a cappella* singing continued to be popular, but after the evolution of polyphonic genres in the Middle Ages—such as organa—Renaissance composers develop new styles of polyphonic and homophonic techniques: for example, the High Renaissance style.

There are a variety of Masses and compositional techniques used by Renaissance composers. Among these are

Sketch of a Renaissance Mass by Albrecht Dürer (1471–1528).

- **Missa brevis**: This means "short Mass." Each section of the Ordinary is much shorter than normal. Sometimes, the Gloria and the Credo (the two Ordinary sections that had the longest text) are left out entirely.
- **Paraphrase Mass**: A Mass in which a preexisting melody is reworked by adding rhythm or extra notes to make it more interesting. Then each section of the Ordinary uses the same melody but paraphrases it slightly differently each time. This provides a musical unity to the Mass. Here is an example of a preexisting plainchant (example 1), followed by the paraphrased version for one of the Ordinary sections of the Mass (example 2).

Example 1: Plainchant

Sal - ve, Re - gi - na

Example 2: Paraphrase of plainchant

Ky - ri - e e - le - i - son, Ky - ri - e e -

Here are both examples again, with lines drawn between to show exactly which notes have been used from the original plainchant in the paraphrase:

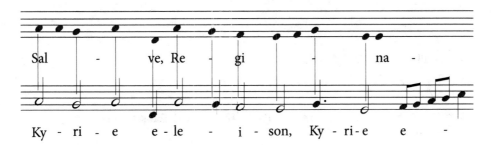

Sal - ve, Re - gi - na -

Ky - ri - e e - le - i - son, Ky - ri - e e -

- **Parody Mass**, or **Imitation Mass**: A Mass in which each Ordinary portion of the Mass begins with (or has a section with) the *exact* same notes in *all* voice parts as a preexisting piece of music. For instance, the first example on the following page is an excerpt from a motet and the second example is an excerpt from a Mass, both of which use identical voicing.

Performing forces for Masses:

Mostly *a cappella* singing.

Compositional techniques used in the Mass in the Renaissance:

- Paraphrase
- Parody
- High Renaissance style

Does the genre of the Mass exist beyond the Renaissance?

Yes. The genre of Mass continues to be a viable music genre to the present day. Masses (or sections from Masses) from the Renaissance are still performed regularly in churches around the world. Masses are composed in subsequent time periods as well, right up to the present day, but the musical style has changed from time period to time period. If you hear a Mass composed in the Baroque Era, it will sound considerably different from a Mass composed in the Renaissance.

FURTHER INVESTIGATION:

1. Listen to a Mass composed in the Renaissance. Notice the texture of the different sections of the Mass to see if the Ordinary sections are more elaborate than the Proper sections. Listen for the High Renaissance style.
2. Listen to a paraphrase Mass after listening to the plainchant or other melody that is being paraphrased so that you'll recognize the paraphrases when you hear them.
3. Listen to a parody Mass after listening to the plainchant or other melody that is being parodied so that you'll recognize the parodied sections when you hear them.

SUGGESTED LISTENING:

- Paraphrase Mass: Josquin Desprez's *Pange lingua Mass*. Listen to a recording of the *Pange lingua* plainchant first, so you can hear what Josquin used as his paraphrase.
- Parody Mass: Josquin's *Missa Malheur me bat*. Listen to Okeghem's chanson *Malheur me bat*, so you can try to hear what was imitated. (Note: This is a bit harder to hear than paraphrase, so you might also need to find a score of each piece to compare back and forth.)
- Missa brevis: Giovanni Pierluigi da Palestrina's *Missa brevis*.

Dance Music

There is a plethora of dance genres in the Renaissance. Some are formal, stately processional-style dances, while others are less-formal folk dances. Here is a list of some of the dances in the Renaissance with a brief description regarding form and style.

- Allemande: Moderate tempo, duple meter
- Basse danse: Stately court dance, sometimes in duple meter, sometimes in triple
- Corrente: A fast dance in triple meter (Italy)
- Courante: Early on, a slow dance in triple meter (France); later, a fast dance in triple meter
- Galliard: Lively with complex choreography, usually triple meter
- Jig: Upbeat, jumping dance, triple (or compound duple) meter (England)
- Pavane: Moderately slow processional dance, duple meter
- Saltarello: Jumping dance, usually in triple meter (Italy)

Nobility dancing the basse danse in the Renaissance.

Performing forces for Renaissance dance music:
Instruments in various combinations.

Does the genre of Renaissance dances exist beyond this Renaissance?
After the Renaissance, many of these dance genres evolved into musical forms intended for listening. Look for the names of Renaissance dances to appear in different genres in future time periods. It is unlikely that composers after the Renaissance had much interest in composing new dances in these specific forms, but you can still see these dances performed regularly at Renaissance fairs, Shakespeare festivals, in period films, etc. There are dance organizations around the world dedicated to teaching and performing Renaissance dance steps.

FURTHER INVESTIGATION:

1. Watch online videos of Renaissance dances to see how they looked and sounded.
2. Search for audio examples of a particular dance type. Most of the results you will find will be from the Renaissance and some will be from subsequent time periods. Listen to examples of Renaissance dances and their counterparts in later time periods to see how they follow a similar form.

SUGGESTED LISTENING:

- Allemande: William Brade's "Allmand No. 2"
- Basse danse: Tylman Susato's *Danse du Roy*
- Corrente: Alessandro Piccinini's "Corrente III" from *Intavolatura di Liuto, et di Chitarrone, Book 1*
- Courante: Jakub Reys' *Courante*
- Galliard: Antony Holborne's *Galliard No. 2*
- Jig: John Dowland's *Tarleton's Jig*
- Pavane: Pierre Phalèse's *Pavane sur la bataille*
- Saltarello: Giorgio Mainerio's *Pass'e mezzo antico and Saltarello*

CHAPTER
NINE
Composers of the Renaissance

Binchois, Gilles (c. 1400–1460)

Country: Holland
Known for: Sacred music
Recommended listening: *Salve Sancta Parens: Introit*

Byrd, William (c. 1540–1623)

Country: England
Known for: Madrigals
Recommended listening: *This sweet and merry month of May*

Dufay, Guillaume (1397–1474)

Country: Holland
Known for: Sacred music
Recommended listening: *Missa Se la face ay pale*

Dunstable, John (c. 1390–1453)

Country: England
Known for: Masses
Recommended listening: *Quam pulchra es* (motet)

Farmer, John (c. 1570-1600)

Country: England
Known for: Madrigals
Recommended listening: *Fair Phyllis I Saw Sitting All Alone*

Gabrieli, Giovanni (c. 1554-1612)

Country: Italy
Known for: Antiphonal Sacred music
Recommended listening: *Jubilate Deo*

The Pardoning of Carlo Gesualdo by Giovanni Balducci (1609); located in the Chiesa Santa Maria delle Grazie, Gesualdo, Italy. Copyright in the Public Domain.

Gesualdo, Carlo (1566-1613)

• After he discovered his wife was having an affair, he had his servants help him kill both her and her lover. He was not prosecuted, most likely because he was a nobleman.[1]

Country: Italy
Known for: Madrigals
Recommended listening: *Gelo ha Madonna il seno*

Isaac, Heinrich (c. 1450-1517)

Country: Netherlands
Known for: Masses
Recommended listening: *Missa de Apostolis*

Janequin, Clement (c. 1485-1558)

Country: France
Known for: Chansons (secular songs)
Recommended listening: *La bataille de Marignan*

---

1   Glenn Watkins, *The Gesualdo Hex: Music, Myth, and Memory* (New York: Norton, 2010), 16–19.

Jeune, Claude le (c. 1530-1600)

Country: France
Known for: Chansons (sacred and secular)
Recommended listening: *Revecy venir du printans*

Josquin des Prez (c. 1450-1521)

Country: France
Known for: Masses
Recommended listening: *Missa Pange lingua*

Lassus, Orlande de (c. 1532-1594)

Country: France
Known for: Motets
Recommended listening: *Prophetiae Sibyllarum*

Marenzio, Luca (c. 1553-1599)

Country: Italy
Known for: Madrigals
Recommended listening: *Leggiadre ninfe e pastorelli amanti*

Morales, Cristóbal de (c. 1500-1553)

Country: Spain
Known for: Masses
Recommended listening: *Missa Benedicta es caelorum regina*

Mouton, Jean (c. 1459-1522)

Country: France
Known for: Masses
Recommended listening: *Ave sanctissima Maria* (motet)

Ockeghem, Johannes (c. 1410–1497)

<u>Country:</u> France
<u>Known for:</u> Masses
<u>Recommended listening:</u> *Missa quinti toni*

Palestrina, Giovanni Pierluigi da (c. 1525–1594)

Portrait of Giovanni Pierluigi da Palestrina.

- He spent most of his life writing sacred music, including masses and motets. He did write some secular music but later said that he repented of it.[2]
- He is often credited for saving church music when the Catholic Church threatened to ban polyphony from the church because they feared it obscured the meaning of the words. Although it has been disproven by musicologists, the legend continues to be perpetuated that he composed a Mass in the High Renaissance style but kept the imitative polyphony to a minimum. Then, when the church leaders heard it, he asked them if they understood all the words. When they responded "yes," he pointed out that it had polyphony in it, so shouldn't be banned.[3]

<u>Country:</u> Italy
<u>Known for:</u> Masses—he wrote over 100 of them.
<u>Recommended listening:</u> *Missa Papae Marcelli*

Tallis, Thomas (c. 1505–1585)

<u>Country:</u> England
<u>Known for:</u> Motets
<u>Recommended listening:</u> *Spem in alium* (a *40* voice motet!)

---

2   Geoffrey Hindley, *Larousse Encyclopedia of Music* (New York: Barnes & Noble, 1994), 129.
3   Piero Weiss and Richard Taruskin, eds., *Music in the Western World: A History in Documents* (New York: Schirmer, 1984), 140–142.

Taverner, John (c. 1490-1545)

Country: England
Known for: Masses
Recommended listening: *"The Western Wind" Mass*

Weelkes, Thomas (1576-1623)

Country: England
Known for: Madrigals
Recommended listening: *Ha ha! This world doth pass*

Wert, Giaches de (1535-1596)

Country: Belgium
Known for: Madrigals
Recommended listening: *Vezzosi augelli*

Willaert, Adrian (c. 1489-1562)

Country: Belgium
Known for: Motets
Recommended listening: *Dilexi, quoniam*

BAROQUE ERA
(1600-1750)

The Baroque Era is a time of great advancement in the amount of music written for orchestral instruments. In the previous time period, most instrumental music was dance music or merely accompaniment for the human voice. In the Baroque Era the focus shifts to instrumental music that is meant to be *listened* to.

Instruments in the Baroque Era

Most of the instruments with which we are familiar today become common in the Baroque Era. Baroque flutes, oboes, bassoons, and the most common brass instruments are simpler than their modern counterparts but essentially sound the same. Baroque string instruments are of an extremely high quality. In fact, string instruments built in the Baroque Era by the famous luthiers Antonio Stradivari and Andrea Guarneri are now worth millions of dollars because of the high quality of their construction. The most common keyboard instrument in the Baroque Era is the harpsichord, but by the mid-1700s, the piano was being perfected and gaining in popularity.

Performance Venues in the Baroque Era

The church and the court continue to be important performance venues in the Baroque Era. In addition, opera houses begin to be built all over Europe. Operas are initially performed in theaters built by the nobility in their homes or on their estates. Only the wealthy and their invited guests are able to experience this new genre. As it becomes more popular, public opera houses offer tickets to the general public. Another important venue in the Baroque Era is the home. Members of the nobility, as well as the general public, perform chamber music in their homes as a form of domestic entertainment.

CHAPTER

TEN

Compositional and Performance Techniques and Forms Used in the Baroque Era

Performance Technique: Basso Continuo

Basso continuo is a technique in which improvised chords are added to the bass line in a piece of music. The chords are improvised by a keyboard player (or guitar-type instrument). The keyboard player is provided with the same bass line as the lower instruments in the performing ensemble (usually cello and bass in an orchestra; cello or bassoon in a chamber ensemble). Based on his/her training, the keyboardist completes, or "realizes," the bass line through improvisation.

This technique makes listening to Baroque music particularly interesting because you will never hear the same piece realized in exactly the same way. Every keyboard player is a unique individual with varied training and experience, so every keyboard player will realize the chords in a slightly different way. Note: any instrument that is assigned to play the bass line is referred to as a continuo player.

Genres that use basso continuo:
- All orchestral genres: Concerto, orchestral suite, sinfonia
- Most vocal genres: Oratorio, cantata, Mass
- Most chamber ensembles

Is basso continuo used in music composed after the Baroque Era?
No. The technique of basso continuo died out after the end of the Baroque Era. It is important to note that when Baroque music is performed nowadays, the existence of basso continuo causes some problems. Keyboardists today are rarely trained to improvise chords based solely on a bass line. As a result, music publishers will often "realize" the bass line for the keyboardists and publish a separate keyboard part with the chords written out. Modern- keyboardists are probably grateful for this.

FURTHER INVESTIGATION:

Listen to three or four recordings of the same piece of Baroque music to see how different the keyboard improvisations can be. To ensure that the recordings are historically accurate, pick performing groups known for historical accuracy, such as Tafelmusik, the Academy of Ancient Music, Concentus Musicus Wien, and the Aulos Ensemble.

Compositional Technique: Figured Bass

Figured bass is a set of symbols written above or below the bass line to help keyboardists realize the bass line. Here's what it looks like on the printed page:

Even though suggested chords are provided by the figured bass, there is still plenty of freedom for the keyboardist to improvise.

Genres that use figured bass:
Any compositions that feature basso continuo can also feature figured bass.

Is figured bass used in music composed after the Baroque Era?
No.

Compositional Technique: Walking Bass

Walking bass is a technique in which every note in the bass line is the same length. Walking bass can be featured throughout an entire piece, or it can be used for sections within a piece (but it has to occur for a fairly long time in order for it to be considered a walking bass). The examples below show a variety of walking bass lines.

Example 1:

Example 2:

Example 3:

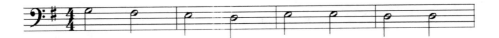

Genres that use walking bass:
It is possible to use walking bass in any genre.

Is walking bass used in music composed after the Baroque Era?
Yes, but not very often in art music. Jazz music uses walking bass frequently.

FURTHER INVESTIGATION:

Look at the scores of at least five different pieces composed in the Baroque Era. Look at the bass line to see if walking bass is used.

SUGGESTED LISTENING:

- Johann Sebastian Bach's "Wiewohl mein Herz in Tränen schwimmt" from *St. Matthew Passion, BWV 244*
- Bach's "Erbarme dich, mein Gott" from *St Matthew Passion, BWV 244*

Compositional Technique: Ground Bass

Ground bass is a bass line in which the succession of pitches (the melody of the bass line) repeat over and over again. Ground bass can be featured throughout an entire piece, or it can be used for sections within a piece. The examples below show a variety of ground bass lines. You can easily see the repetition of each ground bass pattern.

Example 1:

Example 2:

Example 3:

Note that the third example of ground bass is also a walking bass!

Genres that use ground bass:
Composers can use ground bass technique in any genre.

Is ground bass used in music composed after the Baroque Era?
No, not with any regularity. Occasionally, composers in later time periods will use a ground bass for a brief passage within a piece of music, but with less strictness as in the Baroque Era.

SUGGESTED LISTENING:

- Johann Pachelbel's *Canon in D major* (This is undoubtedly the most famous ground bass of all time.)
- Henry Purcell's "When I Am Laid in Earth" from *Dido and Aeneas*.
- Claudio Monteverdi's "Pur ti miro" from Act III of *L'incoronazione di Poppea*.

Form: Fugue

The **fugue** is one of the most popular forms in the Baroque Era. It is highly structured and features almost non-stop imitative polyphony.

The first section of a fugue is called an **exposition**. The exposition begins with the main melody being sounded by a single voice. ("Voice" means either the human voice or an instrumental voice. Most fugues in the Baroque Era are instrumental.) The main melody, stated by Voice One is called the **subject**. The subject is represented in this diagram by a jagged line.

subject

Voice 1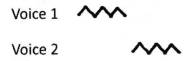

As soon as voice one is finished stating the subject, voice two imitates voice one by restating the subject. The composer can choose to have voice two state the subject at exactly the same pitches as voice one OR at higher or lower pitches than voice one. But regardless of how high or how low voice two is, the subject is recognizable as the same subject with which voice one began the fugue.

Voice 1 ∧∧∧

Voice 2 ∧∧∧

While voice two states the subject, voice one continues with new musical material that sounds good with voice two. This new musical material is represented here by the looped line.

Voice 1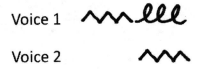

Voice 2 ∧∧∧

Composers can use as many voices as they want in a fugue. The majority of fugues have three or four voices, but they could have as few as two or as many as the composer's skill and imagination can handle.

Every voice in a fugue (regardless of how many) takes a turn stating the subject. Therefore, if it is a three-voice fugue, after voice two states the subject, voice three then states the subject. If it is a four-voice fugue, after voice three states the subject, voice four states the subject. As mentioned above, composers can use as many voices as they feel they can manage.

Even though this is a fairly rigid form, the composer still has opportunities to make creative choices. For instance, when each new voice enters, the composer can have the previous voice state the same new musical material voice one states when voice two begins the subject, as this diagram shows:

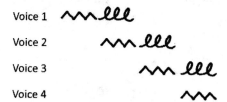

OR, composers can have each new voice introduce completely new musical material when the previous voice states the subject, as this diagram shows:

Voice 1

Voice 2

Voice 3

Voice 4

In addition, the composer can choose to have all voices continue with new musical material, like so:

Voice 1

Voice 2

Voice 3

Voice 4

It is also possible for the composer to have one of the voices drop out for a time.

Another option for the composer is to insert a **bridge** between voices two and three, or between voices three and four, or between voices four and five, etc., like so:

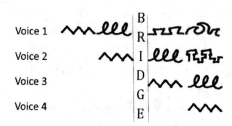

A bridge is extra musical material to stretch the piece out a little bit. The only place a bridge cannot happen is between voices one and two, because if voice two hasn't entered yet, we would assume it is just a really long subject.

When the last voice in a particular fugue finishes stating the subject, the exposition is over and the next part begins. The next part is called an **episode**. In an episode, the composer reworks the material that has already been presented in the exposition.

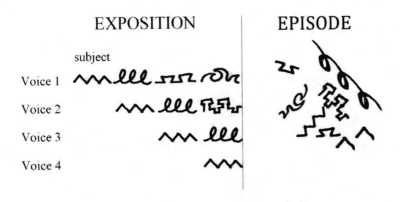

To illustrate the types of things a composer can do to rework the material from the exposition (for use in an episode), here is a sample subject:

Composers use **fugal devices** to create new musical material (for each episode) from the material that already exists (in the exposition). The most commonly used fugal devices are

1. **Retrograde**, or, in other words, backwards.

2. **Inversion** (played upside down):

3. **Retrograde inversion** (upside down and backwards):

4. **Diminution** (making the note values shorter):

5. **Augmentation** (making the note values longer):

6. **Fragmentation** (chopping the musical material up and using only pieces of it):

The principles of all these fugal devices can also be applied to each other: for instance, a retrograde augmented fragment or an inverted diminution. After an episode, the subject returns in its entirety (remember, it *might* have been heard in the episode in a fragmented manner). After it returns, another episode takes place. Then another subject return, another episode, another subject return, and so on, as illustrated here:

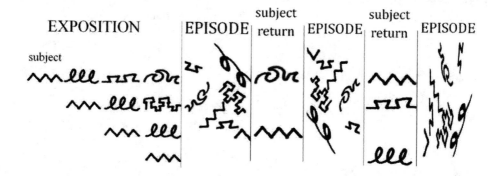

Fugues usually end with a final clear statement of the subject.

Here is the complete exposition of a four-voice fugue—"Contrapunctus I" from *Kunst der Fuge*—by Bach, with each voice labeled.

As you can see, there is no bridge in this exposition—each voice takes a turn stating the subject one after another. Here is "Fugue #5 in D Major" from the *Well-Tempered Klavier* by Bach:

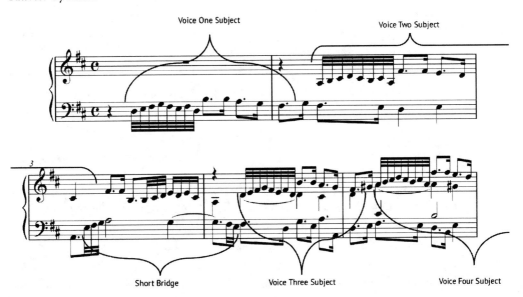

As you can see, in this four-voice fugue, there is a short bridge between voices two and three.

Genres that use fugue form:

A piece written in strict fugue form is referred to as a fugue. In other words, the word "fugue" can be used to denote a genre as well as a form. Most frequently, full fugues are paired with other pieces of music—for example *Toccata and Fugue*, *Fantasia and Fugue*, or *Prelude and Fugue*. You can also find fugal sections within other genres.

Is fugue form used in music composed after the Baroque Era?

Yes, but with considerably less strictness.

FURTHER INVESTIGATION:

1. Listen to a number of Baroque fugues. Try to determine how many voices are in each fugue and whether bridges are used or not.
2. Do a search for "fugue" and the names of subsequent time periods to see how later composers use fugues.

SUGGESTED LISTENING:

- Johann Sebastian Bach's "Fugue #10 in E minor" from the *Well-Tempered Klavier*—it is a two-voice fugue and the subject is quite short.
- Bach's "Fugue #6 in D minor" from the *Well-Tempered Klavier*—three-voice fugue, no bridge.
- Bach's *"Little" Organ Fugue in G Minor, S. 578*—four voices with a really short bridge between voices two and three.
- Bach's "Fugue #22 in F minor" from the *Well-Tempered Klavier*—five voices with a long bridge between voices two and three and a short bridge between voices four and five.

Form: Ritornello

In a piece of music that features **ritornello form,** the initial musical material is presented by a group of instrumentalists—usually a Baroque orchestra (strings and basso continuo). This musical material is called the **ritornello** which means "this music will return again." Following the initial ritornello, a solo section occurs during which the soloist is supported by the other instruments. After the solo section, the ritornello section returns, either in full or in smaller fragments; regardless of the length of the ritornello, it should be enough for the audience to recognize as the material that began the piece. The remainder of the piece alternates between solo sections and ritornello sections for as long as the composer wants.

Although the ritornello sections will all sound familiar due to the repetitive nature of this form, the solo sections are not necessarily based on similar musical material; each solo section can be completely different from the previous solo section if the composer so chooses.

Here is a basic diagram of ritornello form:

Ritornello/Solo 1/Ritornello/Solo 2/Ritornello/Solo 3/Ritornello/Solo 4/ Ritornello/Solo 5/Ritornello/etc.

Genres that use ritornello form:

- Concerto and concerto grosso, usually in the first movement and sometimes in the third movement
- Opera (wherein a vocalist takes the place of the soloist)
- Trio sonata, and other chamber music

Is ritornello form used in music composed after the Baroque Era?

Not really, although later forms may have developed from ritornello form.

Exceptions to the definition above:

Before ritornello form became popular, the word *ritornello* was used to label ANY section of instrumental music that provided a break between numbers in a vocal/ choral work, such as opera, oratorio, or cantata. Don't be surprised if you do a search for ritornello and find a random number in an opera that is only 45 seconds long. The 'return' in such cases is that the ritornello has similar melodic or harmonic elements to the vocal piece that precedes it.

FURTHER INVESTIGATION:

1. Listen to any first movement of a concerto from the Baroque Era. Determine whether or not it follows ritornello form (approximately ninety percent of the time, it will).
2. On a music-streaming website, search the word *ritornello*. Try to find as many different genres that feature ritornello form as possible.

SUGGESTED LISTENING:

- Johann Sebastian Bach's *Brandenburg Concerto #5 in D, BWV 1050*, first movement

- Antonio Vivaldi's *Violin Concerto in B flat, RV 364,* third movement
- Claudio Monteverdi's "Dal mio Permesso amato" from *L'Orfeo*

Form: French Overture

An overture is a piece of music that begins a multi-movement composition or large work like an opera or oratorio. One of the most popular forms for composing an overture in the Baroque Era is **French overture** form. A French overture is an AB form:

> A: A slow opening section with dotted rhythms (a long note followed by a short note—long-short-long-short-long-short)

> B: A faster section featuring imitative polyphony, quite often a fugue.

Genres that use French overture form:
- Suite
- Opera
- Oratorio

Is French Overture form used in music composed after the Baroque Era? Not really, although you can hear its influence on certain overtures of the Classical Era.

FURTHER INVESTIGATION:

Listen to a number of Baroque opera overtures. Try to determine which are in French overture form.

SUGGESTED LISTENING:

- George Frideric Handel's overture to *Water Music Suite in F, HWV 348*
- Henry Purcell's overture to *Dido and Aeneas*
- Handel's overture to *Messiah*

Form: *Da Capo* Aria

A ***da capo*** **aria** is a song in three sections—ABA. The singer sings the first A section then the contrasting B section. The words *da capo* are printed in the music at the end of the B section. *Da capo* means "to the top," so the singer goes back to the beginning and sings the A section again. However, this time the singer improvises extra notes, ornaments, and flashy scales to make it more interesting.

Caricature of a performance of Handel's opera *Flavio*, featuring the soprano Francesca Cuzzoni in the center and the famous (and tall) castrato Senesino on the left; sketch by John Vanderbank (1700's).

Genres that use da capo arias:

- Opera
- Oratorio
- Cantata

Is da capo aria form used in music composed after the Baroque Era?

This form is quite unique to the Baroque Era. There are still plenty of arias written in ABA form up to the present day, but without the improvisation on the second A.

FURTHER INVESTIGATION:

Look at the music for a *da capo* aria to see the indication for *da capo* (or D.C.) at the end of the B section.

SUGGESTED LISTENING:

- George Frideric Handel's "Iris, Hence Away!" from *Semele, HWV 58*
- Handel's "Rejoice Greatly" from *Messiah, HWV 56*
- Johann Sebastian Bach's "Jauchzet Gott in allen Landen!" aria from *Jauchzet Gott in allen Landen!, BWV 51*

Performing Technique: Castrati

Castrati are men who were castrated before puberty in order to prevent their voices from dropping in pitch. Castrati were very popular in Baroque opera. Initially, they played female roles (since the Catholic Church didn't approve of women performing in theatrical productions) but, due to their popularity, castrati eventually performed as the male leading roles. A castrato sounds almost exactly like a female soprano.

Genres that use castrati:

- Opera seria
- Oratorio
- Mass

Were there still castrati after the Baroque Era?

By the end of the Baroque Era, the general public no longer approved of the procedure required to create castrati, thus the use of castrati in opera died out quite quickly. However, castrati continued to sing in church services through the end of the nineteenth century. Nowadays, when an opera company wants to produce a Baroque opera that requires a castrato, they use a countertenor instead.

FURTHER INVESTIGATION:

1. Watch a Baroque opera that features a countertenor in the leading role, for instance *Giulio Cesare* by George Frideric Handel. Note how it seems unusual at first to hear a soprano voice singing the role of the leading male but how, by the end, you become accustomed to it.
2. Search online for and watch videos of countertenors singing Baroque Era music.

SUGGESTED LISTENING:

- Recordings featuring modern-day countertenors David Daniels or Lawrence Zazzo.
- Historical recordings of Alessandro Moreschi, a castrato who lived *just* long enough to see the advent of recording technology.

CHAPTER

ELEVEN

Genres of the Baroque Era

Concerto/Concerto Grosso

A concerto (plural: **concerti**) is an instrumental genre featuring one solo instrument and a Baroque orchestra. The focus is on the interplay between the solo instrument and the orchestra; each vies for our attention in different ways.

A **concerto grosso** (plural: **concerti grossi**) is a concerto that has more than one soloist. Composers write concerti grossi for a small group of soloists, called the *concertino*, and a group of accompanying instruments, called the *ripieno*. The ripieno is usually a full Baroque orchestra, but, depending on the composer and the purpose of the composition, it can also be a smaller group of instruments. Initially, concerti had many movements, but eventually three movements became standard. Generally, the first movement is fast; second is slow; and third is fast.

Performing forces for concerto/concerto grosso:
Generally, a full Baroque orchestra plus soloist(s).

Forms/techniques used in concerti:
- Ritornello form (usually used in the first movement; sometimes in the third).
- **Cadenza:** A moment during a concerto in which the orchestra arrives at a cadential chord and stops playing while the soloist improvises an unaccompanied solo for as long as the soloist deems appropriate. At the end of the improvised cadenza, the orchestra begins playing again to finish the movement.

Does the genre of concerto/concerto grosso exist beyond the Baroque Era?

The genre of concerto, particularly the solo concerto, continued to be popular in subsequent time periods all the way up to and including the present day. The concerto grosso became much less popular after the Baroque Era, but examples of concerti grossi do show up in each of the subsequent time periods.

Exceptions to the definition above:

At an instrumental recital, if a concerto is listed, the assumption is that the performance will feature a solo performer with orchestral accompaniment. However, most solo performers aren't going to go to the effort and expense of hiring a full orchestra for their recital. In these cases, they use what is called a **piano reduction**, or, in other words, a piano arrangement of the orchestral score.

FURTHER INVESTIGATION:

1. Listen to a shuffled playlist of concerti and concerti grossi from the Baroque Era. Try to determine whether each piece is a solo concerto or a concerto grosso.
2. Listen to the first movements of multiple Baroque concerti/concerti grossi and try to determine whether ritornello form is being used or not.

SUGGESTED LISTENING:

- Johann Sebastian Bach's *Brandenburg Concerto #4 in G, BWV 1049*
- Antonio Vivaldi's *Concerto for Mandolin and Strings in C Major, RV 425*
- Georg Philipp Telemann's *Trumpet Concerto in D, TWV 51/D7*

Suite

A **suite** is a multi-movement work in which the first movement is an introduction of sorts (an overture or prelude, for example) and subsequent movements are based on dances. However, suites are not intended for dancing; they are meant for listening pleasure. All the movements in a suite are in the same key. There is no standard number of movements in this genre—it varies widely.

Performing forces for suites:

The genre of the suite is quite versatile; a suite can be composed for a solo instrument, a small group of instruments, or even a full Baroque orchestra. If for a solo instrument, or small group of instruments, the suite is a chamber genre, intended for performance in the home.

Does the genre of suite exist beyond the Baroque Era?

The suite fell out of favor after the Baroque Era for quite some time, but, in the Romantic Era, composers began grouping pieces of instrumental music from various genres together and titled this new grouping a suite. For instance, in the Romantic Era, Georges Bizet wrote the opera *Carmen* and then later selected certain sections of the opera, rewrote them for orchestra (no voice), and grouped them together in a multi-movement suite titled *Carmen Suite*. Tchaikovsky wrote the ballet *Sleeping Beauty* and later selected certain sections from the ballet and grouped them together as *Sleeping Beauty Suite*. In the Twentieth Century, composers created orchestral suites based on a series of related topics: for instance, Gustav Holst's famous suite, *The Planets*, in which each movement is representative of a different planet. In these later suites, the movements were no longer unified by key. In fact, these later suites bear almost no similarity to the suites of the Baroque Era except for the fact that they all have multiple movements.

FURTHER INVESTIGATION:

Listen to a movement of a suite that shares a name with a Renaissance dance form (for instance, allemande or courante), then listen to the Renaissance equivalent to see the evolution from Renaissance to Baroque.

SUGGESTED LISTENING:

- Solo instrument suite: Johann Sebastian Bach's *Cello Suite No. 3 in C major, BWV 1009*
- Keyboard suite: Dietrich Buxtehude's *Suite in D minor, BuxWV 233, "D'amour"*
- Chamber ensemble suite: Marin Marais' "Suite in A minor" from *Pieces de viole, Book 3*
- Orchestral suite: George Frideric Handel's *Music for the Royal Fireworks, HWV 351*

Sonata

The genre of **sonata** is a domestic genre, meaning that sonatas are intended to be played in the home. (This also means that sonatas belong to the larger genre of chamber music.) There is not a standard number of movements in the Baroque sonata, although the most common number is four (slow-fast-slow-fast). Three- and five-movement sonatas are also quite common.

Performance of a flute sonata; note the flute soloist accompanied by basso continuo (harpsichord and low string instrument).

Performing forces for sonatas:

Most sonatas in the Baroque Era are either solo sonatas for one instrument or duo sonatas for one orchestral instrument plus basso continuo.

Does the genre of sonata exist beyond the Baroque Era?

Yes, but not in the exact same way. The use of basso continuo ends with the Baroque Era. And the style of sonatas changes with each new time period.

Exceptions to the above definition:

Sonatas were also performed in church services, most frequently as a substitution for a Proper section of the Mass. These sonatas were often designated as *sonata da chiesa* (church sonata).

FURTHER INVESTIGATION:

Search online for Baroque Era sonatas. Try to find one for unaccompanied solo instrument and one that involves one orchestral instrument plus basso continuo. Listen to them.

SUGGESTED LISTENING:

- Antonio Vivaldi's *Flute Sonata No. 6 in G minor, Op. 13, RV 58, "Il pastor fido"*
- Johann Sebastian Bach's *Violin Sonata No. 1 in G minor, BWV 1001*
- Georg Philipp Telemann's *Recorder Sonata in F Minor, TWV 41:f1*

Trio Sonata

The **trio sonata** is a type of chamber music generally performed in the home. The trio sonata has no specified number of movements, but the most common is a four-movement structure, most often beginning with a slow movement.

Performing forces for trio sonatas:

One might assume that a trio sonata is performed by three musicians, but that is not the case—trio sonatas actually need more than three players: two higher instruments, such as the violin or flute, and one basso continuo part. If the basso continuo is performed in the usual way (keyboard plus low string instrument), this would add up to four performers on three parts. Because this developed as a domestic genre—meaning it was performed in the comfort of one's home by amateur musicians—a lot of the time, the composer wouldn't specify which instruments were to be used. It all depended on which instruments your family or friends played.

Does the genre of trio sonata exist beyond the Baroque Era?

No, it evolved into new genres (such as the piano trio of the next time period) and abandoned the use of the basso continuo.

FURTHER INVESTIGATION:

Watch or listen to (online or live) performances of Baroque trio sonatas to see how they generally require at least four performers.

SUGGESTED LISTENING:

- Jean-Baptiste Loeillet's *Trio Sonata in F major, Op. 2, No. 2*
- Georg Philipp Telemann's *Trio Sonata in C minor, TWV 42:c2*
- George Frideric Handel's *Trio Sonata in G minor, Op. 2, No. 2, HWV 387*

Opera

Opera is a genre in which a story is told through singing and acting, complete with sets and costumes. This genre developed in the latter half of the Renaissance, became very popular among the nobility in the first thirty years of the Baroque Era, and then became available to the general public as opera houses were built all over Europe starting in 1637. Most operas in the early Baroque Era were quite short, often less than an hour, but by the middle of the Baroque Era, operas could last anywhere from an hour to over three hours. To compose an opera, a composer must first obtain a **libretto** from a librettist. A libretto—literally "little book"—is the text for an opera. Some composers worked with the same librettist for years on multiple operas; others worked with different librettists for each opera.

There are two basic types of opera in the Baroque Era—**opera seria** and **opera buffa**.

Opera seria is "serious" opera. The storylines are highly influenced by mythology and/or history, usually telling stories of the triumphs of historical military leaders or royalty. This appealed to members of the nobility of the Baroque Era because they liked to compare themselves to triumphant leaders of the past. In many cases, court composers wrote operas quite overt in the glorification of their employer. The heroes in these operas were sung by the higher voice types—soprano, tenor, and castrato—because the audiences of the day preferred the higher voice to the lower voice.

Opera buffa, on the other hand, is comic opera and was more popular in the public opera houses. The storylines are generally about a servant triumphing over an employer in some way. Nobility are usually depicted as buffoons, sung by the lower voice types—bass and alto. Servants are depicted as wise and kind, sung by the higher voice types—soprano, tenor, and castrato.

Within any opera, there are different kinds of musical numbers. These are called recitative, aria, ensemble, and chorus.

Recitative

A **recitative** is a section within an opera in which narration is sung by a solo singer OR in which dialogue is sung between multiple singers. There are two basic types of recitative—secco and accompanied. Secco means dry. Therefore, **secco recitative** is fairly speech-like (a descendant of recitation) and is accompanied by fairly sparse chords from the continuo players. **Accompanied recitative**, on the other hand, has much more accompaniment from the continuo players and/or orchestra.

Aria

An **aria** is a section within an opera in which a solo singer reflects on a particular plot point, usually focusing on his/her emotions. Arias are highly melodic and highly repetitive; they have solid homophonic accompaniment from the continuo players and/or orchestra. Arias are composed in a number of forms, but *da capo* form was the most popular in the Baroque Era. Arias often use cadenzas.

Ensemble

An **ensemble** (in opera) features more than one singer—mainly duos and trios. This is different from recitative in that it is highly melodic and repetitive like an aria.

Chorus

A **chorus** is a musical number for a larger group of singers, sung in four-part harmony.

Performing forces for opera:
Vocal soloists, chorus, and orchestra.

Forms used in opera:
- *Da capo* aria
- French overture

Does the genre of opera exist beyond the Baroque Era?
Yes, the genre of opera continues to be an important genre to the present day; however, the style changes with each new time period.

Exceptions to the definitions above:
At a vocal recital, if an aria from an opera is listed, the assumption is that the performance would feature a solo singer with orchestral accompaniment. However, most singers, when doing selections from an opera, aren't going to go to the effort and expense of hiring a full orchestra for their recital. Instead, they use a **piano reduction** of the orchestral score.

FURTHER INVESTIGATION:

Watch or listen (online or live) to a Baroque Era opera to see if you can identify the use of and differences between aria, recitative, ensemble, and chorus.

SUGGESTED LISTENING:

- Marc-Antoine Charpentier's *La Descente d'Orphée aux Enfers, H. 488*
- George Frideric Handel's *Giulio Cesare in Egitto, HWV 17*
- Henry Purcell's *Dido and Aeneas*

Oratorio

The genre of **oratorio** is very similar to opera due to the use of recitatives, arias, ensembles, and choruses. An oratorio tells a sacred story, whereas an opera tells a secular story, and oratorios do not use sets or costumes. Oratorios were usually performed as part of a concert series, or in opera houses, for paying audiences.

Performing forces for oratorios:
Vocal soloists, chorus, and orchestra.

Forms used in oratorios:
- *Da capo* aria
- French overture

Does the genre of oratorio exist beyond the Baroque Era?
Yes, the genre of oratorio continued to be quite popular in the next few time periods although the style changed considerably with each new time period. Oratorios are still composed in the present day, though considerably less frequently.

Exceptions to the above definition:
Because oratorios are not performed as part of church services, and are often performed in secular venues, occasionally you will find oratorios with secular subject matter, but these are quite rare.

FURTHER INVESTIGATION:

1. Watch or listen (live or online) to a Baroque Era oratorio to see if you can identify the use of and differences between aria, recitative, ensemble, and chorus.

2. Handel's most famous work, *Messiah*, is perhaps the most-heard oratorio in his-
    tory. It is extremely popular, especially around Christmastime, when professional
    orchestras and choirs offer *Messiah* "sing-alongs" where the audience gets to join
    in on every chorus. Amateur productions also abound using a piano reduction
    or an orchestra made up of whatever instruments the local congregation boasts
    among its membership. Do a quick Internet search of "Messiah sing-along," and
    see what it yields.

SUGGESTED LISTENING:

*   Alessandro Scarlatti's *Agar et Ismaele Esiliati*
*   George Frideric Handel's *Israel in Egypt*
*   Heinrich Schutz's *Historia der frolichen und siegreichen Aufferstehung unsers
    einigen Erlosers und Seligmachers Jesu Christi* (also known as the "Christmas
    Oratorio")

Chorale

A Baroque **chorale** is the same thing as a hymn, similar to those sung in most
Christian churches today—four-part harmony and very homophonic. Chorales
originated in the Lutheran church and were written in the German language. If a
particular chorale was popular, numerous composers would take the chorale tune
(main melody) and write new harmonizations/arrangements of the same chorale
for use in their own compositions. This would be considered plagiarism today, but,
back then, it was considered a compliment if a chorale tune was borrowed by other
composers.

Chorales pretty much always sound like a typical hymn, but sometimes there are
orchestral introductions and interludes between each verse.

Performing forces for chorales:
Soprano, alto, tenor, bass (SATB) or choir with keyboard, chamber, or orchestral
accompaniment/support.

Forms used in chorales:
*   Strophic
*   Ritornello

Does the genre of chorale exist beyond the Baroque Era?

Yes. Even though they originated in the Lutheran church, over the years, other religions borrowed chorales from the Lutheran hymnal, wrote new texts and new harmonizations, and incorporated them into their own hymnals.

FURTHER INVESTIGATION:

Look at the hymnal in a church to see if you can find a hymn attributed to Bach or Martin Luther (both Lutherans). Go to a different Christian church and look in their hymnal to see if you can find the same chorale tunes used.

SUGGESTED LISTENING:

- Johann Sebastian Bach's *Nun danket alle Gott (Now Thank We All Our God)*
- Bach's *Wie soll ich dich empfangen*
- Bach's "Dahero Trotz der Hollen Heer!" from the cantata *Wohl dem, der sich auf seinen Gott, BWV 139*
- *Ein feste Burg ist unser Gott (A Mighty Fortress Is Our God)*—very popular chorale tune attributed to Martin Luther and set (arranged) by numerous composers

Chorale Prelude

A **chorale prelude** is an arrangement of a chorale for solo organ. Despite the fact that the word "chorale" is in the genre title, no singing is involved. Chorale preludes are intended to introduce the hymn tune to the congregation before they sing the chorale as part of the church service.

Performing forces for chorale preludes:
Organ.

Does the genre of chorale prelude exist beyond the Baroque Era?
Yes. Baroque chorale preludes continue to be performed to the present day. Aside from that, any chorale preludes composed in subsequent time periods will feature the stylistic characteristics of their respective time period.

FURTHER INVESTIGATION:

Find some Baroque Era Lutheran chorales that you like. See if there is a chorale prelude version of that same chorale and listen to it.

SUGGESTED LISTENING:

- Johann Sebastian Bach's *Nun danket Alle Gott, BWV 657*
- Bach's *Wachet auf, ruft uns die Stimme, BWV 645*
- Bach's *Herzlich tut mich verlangen, BWV 727*

Cantata

A **cantata** is a sacred, dramatic, relatively-short musical presentation (similar to oratorio) performed in the Lutheran church service. Because it has to fit within the confines of a typical Lutheran church service, the length of a cantata is usually between fifteen and thirty minutes. Cantatas, like oratorios, feature recitatives, arias, and choruses and do not use sets, acting, or costumes. The choruses used in a cantata are chorales, performed as a simple hymn or elaborated upon with lots of orchestral interludes.

Performing forces for cantatas:
Vocal soloists, choir, organ, continuo, orchestra.

Does the genre of cantata exist beyond the Baroque Era?
Yes. After the Baroque Era, other religions borrowed the genre, and you can find cantatas written by many composers in many religions, but the style changes with each new time period.

FURTHER INVESTIGATION:

1. Watch or listen to a Baroque Era cantata to see how the choruses (chorales) are different from opera choruses.
2. Watch or listen to a Baroque Era cantata to see how aria and recitative function in a similar manner as in opera.

SUGGESTED LISTENING:

- Johann Sebastian Bach's *Ein feste Burg ist unser Gott, BWV 80*
- Bach's *Lobe den Herren, den mächtigen König der Ehren, BWV 137*
- Bach's *Herz und Mund und Tat und Leben, BWV 147*

Mass

The Mass as a genre is still alive and well in the Baroque Era. It is used in both the Catholic and Lutheran churches, and the only real difference is that the musical style changed from the High Renaissance style to a much more Baroque style.

FURTHER INVESTIGATION:

Watch or listen to a Mass from the Renaissance and a Mass from the Baroque Era. Note the differences in style.

SUGGESTED LISTENING:

- Johann Sebastian Bach's *Mass in B minor, BWV 232*
- Johann David Heinichen's *Mass No. 11 in D major*
- Johann Ernst Eberlin's *Mass No. 34 in C major*

CHAPTER TWELVE
Composers of the Baroque Era

Albinoni, Tomaso (1671–c. 1750)

- He is best known for a piece of music he didn't even compose. For a good portion of the Twentieth Century, the listening public was entranced by *Adagio in G minor*, purportedly discovered by musicologist Remo Giazotto shortly after World War II. After much scholarly research, the majority opinion is that the piece was entirely composed by Giazotto and has no connection to Albinoni.[1]

Country: Italy
Known for: Concerti
Recommended listening: *Concerto a 5 in G minor, Op. 10, No. 2*

Aubert, Jacques (1689–1753)

Country: France
Known for: Concerti
Recommended listening: *Concerto No. 3 in D Major, Op. 26*

Bach, Johann Sebastian (1685–1750)

- He spent most of his life working in the Lutheran church.
- He wrote some of the best-known secular keyboard music in the world, notably *The Well-Tempered Klavier.*

---

1 Michael Talbot, *Tomaso Albinoni: The Venetian Composer and His World* (New York: Oxford, 1990), v.

Johann Sebastian Bach

- He was not famous as a composer in his lifetime. Almost 80 years after his death, Romantic Era–composer Felix Mendelssohn produced a performance of Bach's *St. Matthew Passion*, which began a Bach revival. Bach has become continually more famous with each passing year.[2]
- He went blind in the last ten years of life.[3]

<u>Country:</u> Germany
<u>Known for:</u> Cantatas, Concerti, Keyboard music
<u>Recommended listening:</u> *Was mir behagt, ist nur die muntre Jagd, BWV 208*, "*Hunt Cantata*," especially the fourth aria, "Schafe konnen sicher weiden"

Biber, Heinrich I. F. von (1644-1704)

<u>Country:</u> Germany
<u>Known for:</u> Violin Sonata
<u>Recommended listening:</u> *Passacaglia in G Minor*

Boismortier, Joseph B. de (1689-1755)

<u>Country:</u> France
<u>Known for:</u> Flute Sonatas
<u>Recommended listening:</u> *Flute Sonata in E Minor, Op. 91, No. 4*

Buxtehude, Dietrich (c. 1637-1707)

<u>Country:</u> Denmark
<u>Known for:</u> Organ music
<u>Recommended listening:</u> *Prelude and Fugue in F-Sharp Minor, BuxWV 146*

Charpentier, Marc-Antoine (1643-1704)

<u>Country:</u> France
<u>Known for:</u> Sacred music, Opera
<u>Recommended listening:</u> *La Descente d'Orphee aux Enfers H. 488*, particularly "Je ne refuse point le secours" from Act II, scene 2.

---

2   John Eliot Gardiner, *Bach: Music in the Castle of Heaven* (New York: Random, 2013), 344.
3   Klaus Eidam, *The True Life of Johann Sebastian Bach* (New York: Basic, 1999), 345–346.

Corelli, Arcangelo (1653-1713)

Country: Italy
Known for: Trio sonatas
Recommended listening: *Sonata da Chiesa in G Major, Op. 1, No. 9*

Couperin, François (1668-1733)

Country: France
Known for: Keyboard music
Recommended listening: *Les ombres errantes* from Pieces de Clavecin, Book Four

Fasch, Johann Friedrich (1688-1758)

Country: Germany
Known for: Concerti
Recommended listening: *Concerto for Two Oboes and Bassoon in C Minor, FWV L:c2*

Fux, Johann Joseph (1660-1741)

Country: Austria
Known for: Sacred vocal music
Recommended listening: *Partita No. 5 in C Major, K323* (violin music)

Graupner, Christoph (1683-1760)

Country: Germany
Known for: Orchestral suites
Recommended listening: *Suite for Flute, Viola d'Amore, 2 Chalumeaux and Horn in F Major, GWV 451*

Guerre, Élisabeth Jacquet de la (1665-1729)

Country: France
Known for: Keyboard suites
Recommended listening: *Harpsichord Suite No. 5 in D Minor*

George Frideric Handel

Handel, George Frideric (1685-1759)

- He spent most of his life working in the secular world, particularly in the genres of opera seria and oratorio.[4]
- During a duel, his opponent's sword broke when it hit Handel's coat button, thus saving Handel's life.[5]

<u>Country:</u> Germany
<u>Known for:</u> Oratorios, Opera
<u>Recommended listening:</u> *Israel in Egypt*, particularly "He Led Them Forth like Sheep"

Hasse, Johann Adolph (1699-1783)

<u>Country:</u> Germany
<u>Known for:</u> Opera seria
<u>Recommended listening:</u> *Artaserse*, particularly "Va' tra le selve ircane"

Hotteterre, Jacques-Martin (1673-1763)

<u>Country:</u> France
<u>Known for:</u> Flute music
<u>Recommended listening:</u> *Trio Sonata in G Major, Op. 3, NO. 6*

Legrenzi, Giovanni (1626-1690)

<u>Country:</u> Italy
<u>Known for:</u> Sonatas
<u>Recommended listening:</u> *La cetra, Op. 10, Book 4: Sonata terza a 4*

Locatelli, Pietro (1695-1764)

<u>Country:</u> Italy
<u>Known for:</u> Violin music
<u>Recommended listening:</u> *Violin Concerto in A Major, Op. 3, No. 11*

---

4   Donald Burrows, ed., *The Cambridge Companion to Handel* (Cambridge: Cambridge, 1997), xi–xvi.
5   R. A. Streatfeild, *Handel* (New York: Da Capo Press, 1964), 19.

Loeillet, Jacques (1685-1748)

<u>Country:</u> Belgium
<u>Known for:</u> Oboe music
<u>Recommended listening:</u> *Oboe Concerto in E-Flat Major*

Loeillet, Jean-Baptiste (1688-1720)

<u>Country:</u> Belgium
<u>Known for:</u> Recorder music
<u>Recommended listening:</u> *Recorder Sonata in D Minor, Op. 2, No. 3*

Lully, Jean-Baptiste (1632-1687)

- He worked as a court composer for King Louis XIV of France and wrote a number of ballets in which Louis XIV was the lead dancer.[6]
- He suffered an unusual death. Lully was conducting a performance of one of his sacred works using his cane to keep time. He accidentally brought the staff down on one of his feet, stabbing it; it subsequently developed gangrene, and he died from the infection.[7]

<u>Country:</u> Born in Italy; lived primarily in France
<u>Known for:</u> Opera
<u>Recommended listening:</u> "Air pour les Mesmes" from *Le mariage force* (ballet)

Jean-Baptiste Lully

Marais, Marin (1656-1728)

<u>Country:</u> France
<u>Known for:</u> Chamber music
<u>Recommended listening:</u> *Sonnerie de Sainte Genevieve du Mont de Paris*

---

6   Rebecca Harris-Warrick and Carol G. Marsh, *Musical Theatre at the Court of Louis XIV* (Cambridge: Cambridge, 1994), 10.
7   John Hajdu Heyer, ed. *Jean-Baptiste Lully and the Music of the French Baroque* (Cambridge: Cambridge, 1989), 81.

Marcello, Benedetto (1686-1739)

Country: Italy
Known for: Cantata
Recommended listening: *Senza gran pena* (a secular solo cantata)

Molter, Johann-Melchior (1696-1765)

Country: Germany
Known for: Concerti
Recommended listening: *Clarinet Concerto No. 4 in D Major* (These concerti were composed at a time when the clarinet was only just barely invented!)

Pachelbel, Johann (1653-1706)

- His most famous composition—*Canon in D*—is so ubiquitous it has eclipsed all his other music. This single piece, originally for three violins and basso continuo, has been arranged for practically every combination of instruments. It is played at weddings, used in advertising and film, and has been parodied on YouTube, on television shows, and in other compositions. It is a shame he has become known as a "one-hit wonder" because, in fact, he wrote a lot of music worthy of consideration.[8]

Country: Germany
Known for: Chamber music
Recommended listening: *Partita No. 2 in C Minor*

Pergolesi, Giovanni Battista (1710-1736)

Country: Italy
Known for: Opera buffa
Recommended listening: *La serva padrona*

Purcell, Henry (1659-1695)

Country: England
Known for: Opera
Recommended listening: *Dido and Aeneas*

---

8 Jim Svejda, *The Record Shelf Guide to Classical CDs and Audiocassettes* (Rocklin, CA: Prima, 1996), 517.

Quantz, Johann Joachim (1697-1773)

<u>Country:</u> Germany
<u>Known for:</u> Flute music
<u>Recommended listening:</u> *Flute Concerto in A Minor, QV 5:238*

Rameau, Jean-Philippe (1683-1764)

<u>Country:</u> France
<u>Known for:</u> Opera seria
<u>Recommended listening:</u> *Castor et Pollux*

Sammartini, Giuseppe (1695-1750)

<u>Country:</u> Italy
<u>Known for:</u> Concerti
<u>Recommended listening:</u> *Recorder concerto in F Major*

Scarlatti, Domenico (1685-1757)

<u>Country:</u> Italy
<u>Known for:</u> Keyboard sonatas
<u>Recommended listening:</u> *Keyboard Sonata in G Major, K. 146*

Strozzi, Barbara (1619-1677)

<u>Country:</u> Italy
<u>Known for:</u> Vocal music
<u>Recommended listening:</u> *Arie a voce sola, Op. 8*, especially "Luci belle deh ditemi perche"

Tartini, Giuseppe (1692-1770)

<u>Country:</u> Italy
<u>Known for:</u> Violin music
<u>Recommended listening:</u> *Violin Sonata in G Minor ("The Devil's Trill")*

Telemann, Georg Philipp (1681-1767)

Country: Germany
Known for: Concerti
Recommended listening: *Concerto for Recorder and Oboe in F Major, TWV 54:F1*

Torelli, Giuseppe (1658-1709)

Country: Italy
Known for: Concerti
Recommended listening: *Concerto Grosso in E Minor, Op. 8, No. 9*

Caricature of Antonio Vivaldi. This is the only known representation of Vivaldi that was created in his lifetime. All other paintings that feature Vivaldi were created much later.
Copyright in the Public Domain

Vivaldi, Antonio (1678-1741)

- Most of his career was spent at the Ospedale della Pietà, an orphanage/school for girls. He was able to experiment and create his music with a built-in set of musicians ready to play for him.[9]
- He wrote over forty operas, yet they are rarely performed today. His orchestral compositions are so popular they overshadow his operas.[10]

Country: Italy
Known for: Concerti
Recommended listening: *Concerto in A Minor for 2 Oboes & Strings, RV 536*

---

9   Walter Kolneder, *Antonio Vivaldi: His Life and Work* (Los Angeles: University of California Press, 1970), 10–17.
10   Michael Collins and Elise K. Kirk, eds., *Opera & Vivaldi* (Austin: University of Texas Press, 1984), 2.

CLASSICAL ERA (1750-1830)

The music of the Classical Era focuses on entertainment. Classical composers want audiences to leave at the end of a concert humming the tunes. Because of this, there is a definite shift toward homophonic music that allows the main melody to be the focal point. Polyphony is still used in the Classical Era, but less so than in the previous era.

Instruments in the Classical Era

Woodwind, brass, string, and keyboard instruments continue to be used and perfected during the Classical Era. In addition to the flute, oboe, and bassoon, the clarinet becomes a part of the orchestra. The most common keyboard instrument in the Classical Era is the piano. The harpsichord is no longer an essential part of the orchestra but continues to be used, mainly in secco recitative sections in operas.

Performance Venues in the Classical Era

The church, court, opera house, and private home continue to be important performance venues in the Classical Era. In addition, concert halls become more common to showcase the rising genre of the symphony and to make orchestral music more accessible to the general public.

CHAPTER

THIRTEEN

Forms Used in the Classical Era

Many composers in the Classical Era felt the pressure of working for demanding patrons who expected new compositions almost on a daily basis. To alleviate this stress, composers relied on tried-and-true compositional forms to help them compose music with greater ease.

Form: Sonata

Sonata form is the most popular form of the Classical Era. If listeners understand this form, even at its most basic, their enjoyment of music will increase; literally hundreds of compositions from this time period employ sonata form.

Sonata form can be diagrammed with a large ABA structure. The first A section is called the **exposition**. The B section is called the **development**. And the final A section is called the **recapitulation** and might be labeled with a prime, because, even though it is a repeat of the first A section, there are some pretty substantial changes.

The exposition "exposes" all the musical material that will be used for the remainder of the composition. Here is the order in which things occur in the exposition:

1. **First theme:** The first theme is usually a fairly simple melody with homophonic support in the tonic key. Occasionally, composers make the first theme a little more elaborate, but usually it is quite hummable.
2. **Bridge:** A bridge can be quite melodic or merely functional. Its purpose is to transition the composition from the tonic key to a closely related key (like the dominant). This closely related key can be higher or lower than the tonic key—whatever the composer wants.

3. **Second theme:** Another fairly simple melody in the new key.
4. **Cadence theme:** Yet another fairly simple melody, also in the new key, but this one ends with a solid cadential chord. A listener might be convinced that it is the end of the piece—that's how conclusive the cadential chord at the end of the cadence theme can sound. But it is not the end of the piece; it is only the end of the exposition.

The development is a contrasting section (B) to the exposition. In the development, the composer takes musical material from the exposition and reworks or develops it. There isn't a set pattern for the development—composers can fragment motives from the exposition, draw them out, elaborate upon them, etc. (This is reminiscent of the episode in a fugue.) The only thing all developments have in common is modulation. At the end of the development, there is a feeling of suspense; the music sounds like it is heading somewhere. This moment is called the **retransition**. Its purpose is to prepare for the return of the tonic. Earlier, the bridge functioned as a transition from the tonic key to a new key. The retransition now takes the piece back to the tonic key and to the third section of sonata form.

The recapitulation (A) begins with the first theme from the exposition because, as previously mentioned, the recapitulation is a repeat of the exposition—first theme, bridge, second theme, and cadence theme all occur again. The difference this time is that it all stays in the tonic key. The bridge no longer serves its original function. Because the original purpose of the bridge was to modulate from one key to another, the composer has to rework the way the bridge sounds; the composer may have to quickly modulate through a few keys to force the bridge to end up back in the tonic key so that the remainder of the recapitulation stays in the tonic key.

Here's what it looks like all put together:

A	Exposition	First theme • Hummable melody • In the tonic key Bridge • Modulates the piece to a new key Second theme • New melodic material • In the new key Cadence theme • New melodic material • Stays in the new key • Ends with a final-sounding cadence

B	Development	Reworking earlier material • Lots of modulation • Usually quite polyphonic Retransition • Sounds like it is leading to something important • Takes the piece back to tonic key
A	Recapitulation	First theme • In the tonic key Bridge • Remains in the tonic key Second theme • Remains in the tonic key Cadence theme • Remains in the tonic key

There are three optional elements a composer *can* use in sonata form.

1. **Coda:** Composers can add a coda at the end of the recapitulation. The word "coda" means "tail." The purpose of a coda is to extend the final cadence theme and make it feel extremely conclusive. Often the coda repeats the tonic many times to really pound it into the listener that the piece has arrived "home."

2. **Repeat of the exposition:** Composers can insert a repeat sign at the end of the exposition. A repeat sign indicates that the performers should repeat the entire exposition, note for note. Sometimes this can sound jarring because the piece jumps from the new key (at the end of the exposition) to the tonic key.

3. **Slow introduction:** Composers can use a slow introduction before the exposition. There is no rule as to how long or short this slow introduction should be. Some composers use very lengthy slow introductions, others use very short introductions, and, since this is an optional element, many composers don't use a slow introduction at all.

Genres that use sonata form:

Any genre can use sonata form. Opera overtures, orchestral music, chamber music—all regularly feature sonata form. Sonata form was so popular in the Classical Era that composers used it for any movement in any genre they wanted. It was most commonly used in the first movement.

Is sonata form used in music composed after the Classical Era?

Yes, to a degree. All composers from the Baroque Era onward are taught sonata form, but in subsequent time periods, the form is frequently altered by composers in ways that make it much less obvious to the listener. You should not assume that you will hear sonata form in later time periods as frequently as you will in music from the Classical Era.

FURTHER INVESTIGATION:

Listen to practically any first movement of any genre in the Classical Era and try to follow along with sonata form.

SUGGESTED LISTENING:

- Wolfgang Amadeus Mozart's *Don Giovanni, Overture*. Note: This features a slow intro.
- Mozart's *Eine kleine Nachtmusik, first movement*. Well known and relatively easy to follow.
- Mozart's *Piano Sonata #18 in D, K 576, "Hunt," first movement*. Not only is there a strong cadence at the end of the cadence theme, but there's also a cadence at the end of the bridge, so don't let that fool you.
- Mozart's *Piano Sonata #5 in G, K 283, first movement*. There is a fairly solid cadence at the end of the first theme, but it is followed by a fairly obvious bridge, a very pretty second theme, and a long cadence theme.

Form: Variation

Variation form is a form that begins with a theme (or main melody) which is followed by numerous variations on the theme. This can be diagrammed as:

A	A'	A''	A'''	A''''	A'''''	A''''''	A'''''''
(Theme)	(Var. 1)	(Var. 2)	(Var. 3)	(Var. 4)	(Var. 5)	(Var. 6)	(Var. 7)

There are many ways to create variations of a theme. The melody can be ornamented, paraphrased, assigned new rhythms, and changed from major to minor; the harmony can be varied as well. The possibilities are endless, and composers can write as many variations as they want (or as will keep the audience's attention).

Each section within variation form can be diagrammed more specifically as well. This chart shows the most common ways Classical Era composers organize themes and variations. Note: the vertical lines with the two dots is a "repeat sign"—anything between the dots is repeated.

	A	A'	A"
Possibility #1	|:a:||:b:|	|:a':||:b':|	|:a":||:b":|
Possibility #2	|:a:||:ba:|	|:a':||:b'a':|	|:a":||:b"a":|
Possibility #3	|:a:||:ba':|	|:a":||:b'a'":|	|:a'''':||:b"'a'''':|

Notice in Possibility #3 that the first little "a" is changed slightly in the second part of the theme, which is why it has a prime. Composers can use one of the above possibilities for the theme and then one of the other possibilities for the first variation and then a completely different one for the second variation; composers can also fragment any of the above options or leave out repeats, like this example:

A	A'	A"	A'''	A''''	A'''''
|:a:||:ba:|	a'b'a'	|:a":||:b"a":|	a'''b'''	|:a'''':|	|:a''''':||:b'''''a''''':|

Genres that use variation form:
- Any genre can use variation form.
- Used most frequently in:
  - Symphony
  - Sonata
  - Chamber music
  - Solo piano music

Is variation form used in music composed after the Classical Era?
Yes, variation form continues to be popular to the present day. The style, however, changes with each time period. Variation form was particularly popular in the Romantic Era as virtuosic, stand-alone pieces of music for solo instruments (accompanied by piano or orchestra).

FURTHER INVESTIGATION:

1. Listen to variations from the Classical Era. Pay close attention to the theme to determine which diagram to use to follow along. See if each variation follows the same diagram or alters it slightly (or hugely).

2. Listen to variations with a score in front of you to follow along. (Being able to see the repeat signs printed in the score will help.)
3. Listen to variations without a score and count how many variations you hear.

SUGGESTED LISTENING:

* Wolfgang Amadeus Mozart's *12 Variations in C Major, on "Ah, vous dirai-je maman," K. 265*
* Franz Joseph Haydn's *Symphony No. 31 in D major, Hob1:31, "Horn Signal"* (fourth movement)
* Haydn's *Symphony No. 94 in G major, Hob.I:94, "The Surprise"* (second movement)

Form: Minuet

Minuet form evolved from a Baroque Era dance called the "minuet." The Baroque dance minuet was in triple meter and had a middle section of contrasting music called a trio. The basic structure of Classical Era minuet form—also in triple meter—is

A   B   A

Minuet Trio Minuet

The large letters—ABA—can also be sub-divided, like so:

	A	B	A
Possibility #1	|: a :| |: ba :|	|: c :| |: dc :|	aba

Composers also use primes within the basic structure wherever they deem appropriate. Here are a few of the possibilities:

	A	B	A
Possibility #2	|: a :| |: ba' :|	|: c :| |: dc' :|	aba'
Possibility #3	|: a :| |: ba' :|	|: c :| |: dc :|	aba'
Possibility #4	|: a :| |: ba :|	|: c :| |: dc' :|	aba

It is also quite common for the trio section to be a different tempo from the minuet sections. This is one of the easiest forms to follow in all of music history. Each phrase is relatively short, and all the repetition helps orient the listener.

Genres that use minuet form:

- Any instrumental genre in the Classical Era can use minuet form.
- Used most frequently in:
  - Symphony
  - String quartet
  - Wind quintet

Is minuet form used in music composed after the Classical Era?

Yes, but much less frequently, much less rigidly adhered to, and, of course, changed to fit the style of each new time period.

FURTHER INVESTIGATION:

1. Listen to Classical Era pieces in minuet form (found most frequently in the third movement of practically any Classical Era symphony or string quartet). Use the diagram above to follow along.
2. Look at instrumental scores of pieces in minuet form. Notice how repeat signs are used in the printed music, as well as the term *da capo* or its abbreviation "D.C."

SUGGESTED LISTENING:

- Johann Baptist Vanhal's *Symphony in G minor, Bryan Gm2* (third movement)
- Franz Danzi's *Wind Quintet in B flat major, Op. 56, No. 1* (third movement)
- Wolfgang Amadeus Mozart's *Serenade No. 13 in G major, K. 525, "Eine kleine Nachtmusik"* (third movement)

Form: Scherzo

Various composers began replacing minuet form with **scherzo** near the end of the Classical Era. Beethoven was the most influential in this change. It is certainly possible to find a minuet in one of Beethoven's multi-movement instrumental works, but the scherzo is much more frequent. Scherzo form follows the same diagram as minuet form, but there are a few differences:

- The scherzo is much faster than the minuet, which means that the triple meter is sped up considerably (so that dancing to it would be quite awkward).
- There is more freedom with the form, for instance the second "a" in the first section can be considerably altered or extended (more than would have occurred in minuet form).

Genres that use scherzo:

• Symphony
• String quartet
• Other chamber music

Is scherzo form used in music composed after the Classical Era?

Yes. Because this was popularized by Beethoven near the end of the Classical Era, it continued into the Romantic Era for some time. The form became more and more free as time went on. In the Romantic Era and thereafter, many composers titled pieces or movements as "scherzo" with the only connection to the Classical Era scherzo being the tempo—all scherzo pieces have a fast tempo.

FURTHER INVESTIGATION:

1. Listen to a number of scherzo movements from the Classical Era to see if they follow the form or if they take liberties
2. Listen to a number of pieces titled "scherzo" from the Romantic Era to the present day and see how they differ from the scherzo form of the Classical Era.

SUGGESTED LISTENING:

• Ludwig van Beethoven's *Symphony No. 2 in D major, Op. 36* (third movement)
• Beethoven's *String Quartet No. 2 in G major, Op. 18, No. 2* (third movement)
• Beethoven's *Piano Sonata No. 15 in D major, Op. 28, "Pastoral"* (third movement)

Form: Rondo

Rondo form is the form that allows Classical Era composers the most freedom. Rondo form can be diagrammed in any of the following ways (and many more):

ABABA

ABACA

ABACABA

ABACADABA

And so on and so on ...

The one obvious connection between all these possible diagrams is that the A section is repeated numerous times. This form is likely a further evolution of ritornello form.

The most common diagram for rondo form is

ABACA

As with previous forms in this chapter, each capital letter in the diagram *can* also be sub-divided, like so:

	A	B	A	C	A
Possibility #1	|:a:||:b:|	|:c:||:d:|	|:a:||:b:|	|:e:||:f:|	|:a:||:b:|
Possibility #2	|:a:||:ba:|	|:c:||:dc:|	|:a:||:ba:|	|:e:||:fe:|	|:a:||:ba:|

Also, as with earlier forms in this chapter, composers can choose to use |:a:||:ba:| for the first large A, but then use |:a:||:b:| for the second large A, or vice versa, or they may choose to leave the repeats out for one or more of the larger sections. They may even extend, shorten, or alter (prime) any of the sections at will. It is generally easier to follow along with the larger letters than the subdivisions.

Genres that use rondo form:
- Symphony
- Sonata
- Concerto
- String quartet
- Other chamber music

Is rondo form used in music composed after the Classical Era?
Yes, but as with other Classical Era forms, the form is much freer in subsequent time periods.

FURTHER INVESTIGATION:

1. Listen to recordings of Classical Era pieces in rondo form (often the final movement of any instrumental genre). See if you can follow the overall form (usually ABACA) first. Then see if you can determine if each big letter is divided into smaller letters.
2. Listen to the last movement of a few Classical Era concerti. Notice that in most large-lettered sections, when the little letters repeat, the first time features the soloist and the second time features the orchestra.

SUGGESTED LISTENING:

- Ludwig van Beethoven's *Bagatelle in A minor, WoO 59, "Für Elise"* (ABACA)
- Wolfgang Amadeus Mozart's *Clarinet Concerto in A major, K. 622,* third movement (ABACABA)
- Franz Joseph Haydn's *Symphony No. 68 in B flat major, Hob.I:68,* fourth movement (ABACADA+Coda)

Form: Sonata-Rondo

As can be assumed from its name, this is a hybrid of sonata form and rondo form. This diagram shows traditional sonata form on the left and **sonata-rondo form** on the right.

SONATA FORM		SONATA-RONDO FORM	
		A	first theme (tonic)
A Exposition	First theme / Bridge / Second theme / Cadence theme	B	second theme (dominant)
		A	first theme (tonic)
B Development	Rework earlier material / Retransition	C	Development
		A	first theme (tonic)
A Recapitulation	First theme / Bridge / Second theme / Cadence theme	B	second theme (tonic)
		A	first theme (tonic)

It is easy to see the relationship between both sonata and rondo form in this hybrid form. It is also easy to see how one might mistake sonata-rondo form for rondo form. To make matters even more confusing, sometimes when composers title a movement with the word "rondo," it is actually in sonata-rondo form.

<u>**Genres that use sonata-rondo form:**</u>

- Symphony
- Concerto
- Sonata
- String quartet
- Other chamber music

<u>**Is sonata-rondo form used in music composed after the Classical Era?**</u>

Yes, but not nearly as much as in the Classical Era, and as with other Classical Era forms, it is much freer in subsequent time periods.

FURTHER INVESTIGATION:

Do an online search for Classical Era compositions in sonata-rondo form. Listen to them and follow along with the diagram.

SUGGESTED LISTENING:

- Wolfgang Amadeus Mozart's *Serenade No. 13 in G major, K. 525, "Eine kleine Nachtmusik"* (fourth movement)
- Franz Joseph Haydn's *Symphony No. 103 in E flat major, Hob.I:103, "Drumroll"* (fourth movement)
- Haydn's *Symphony No. 100 in G major, Hob.I:100, "Military"* (fourth movement)

CHAPTER FOURTEEN
Genres of the Classical Era

Symphony

A **symphony** is a multi-movement work for orchestra. The traditional number of movements is four.

The symphony developed out of the orchestral music of the previous time period. Orchestral suites, "sinfonias" (orchestral music within a Baroque opera, oratorio, or cantata), and concerti all had an influence on the development of this genre. The symphony flourished in the Classical Era with the expanding popularity and availability of public concert halls. Because the symphony swiftly became the orchestral genre of choice, orchestras began to be referred to as "symphony orchestras."

Each movement in the symphony has certain characteristics that remain fairly constant throughout this time period.

The first movement is generally 1) fast, 2) of a serious nature, and 3) in sonata form.

The second movement is generally 1) slow, 2) meant to be beautiful, and 3) in whatever form the composer preferred.

The third movement is generally 1) light in mood, 2) dance-like, and 3) in minuet form.

The fourth movement is generally 1) the fastest of the movements, 2) of a playful nature, and 3) in rondo form.

Occasionally the second and third movements swap positions. And because sonata form is so popular in this time period, it is often used for both the first AND fourth movements.

Performing forces for the genre of symphony:
A Classical Era orchestra.

Forms used in symphonies:

*   sonata form
*   variation form
*   minuet form
*   scherzo form
*   rondo form
*   sonata-rondo form

Does the genre of symphony exist beyond the Classical Era?
Yes. The symphony continues to be a vital genre to the present day, but the style changes with each time period.

Exceptions to the definition above:
Prior to the Classical Era, the word "symphony" meant something else. Do not be surprised if you see the word "symphony" or some variant of it used in a different way in earlier time periods.

FURTHER INVESTIGATION:

1. Create a playlist featuring nothing but Classical Era symphonies. Set the playlist to "shuffle" and without looking at the titles, try to figure out which movement you are listening to, based on the general characteristics of each movement.
2. Watch or listen to an entire Classical Era symphony. Note the stylistic features of the Classical Era.

SUGGESTED LISTENING:

*   Franz Joseph Haydn's *Symphony No. 94 in G major, Hob.I:94, "The Surprise"*
*   Wolfgang Amadeus Mozart's *Symphony No. 41 in C major, K. 551, "Jupiter"*
*   Ludwig van Beethoven's *Symphony No. 1 in C major, Op. 21*

Concerto

The Classical concerto is similar to the Baroque concerto in that it is a composition for a soloist with orchestra. Concerti grossi are not as popular in the Classical Era as they were in the previous era, partly because the focus of the Classical Era is on melody, not polyphony.

Each movement in the concerto has certain characteristics that remain fairly constant throughout this time period.

The first movement is generally 1) fast, 2) of a serious nature, and 3) in sonata form. One important note about the first movement of a concerto is that the treatment of sonata form is very different from the treatment in other genres. In other genres, the exposition can be repeated if the composer wants to do so. In concerti, the repeated exposition is practically guaranteed to happen. It is not merely an optional choice. The exposition is first presented by the orchestra alone and then is repeated with the soloist as the main focus (with orchestral support).

The second movement is generally 1) slow, 2) meant to be beautiful, and 3) in whatever form the composer prefer.

The third movement is generally 1) the fastest of the movements, 2) of a playful nature, and 3) in rondo form.

Note that, unlike the symphony, concerti do not use minuet form.

Performing forces for concerti:
Solo instrument plus Classical orchestra.

Forms used in concerti:
*   Sonata form (with repeated exposition; first one for orchestra, second for soloist with orchestral support)
*   Variation form
*   Rondo form
*   Sonata-rondo form

Technique used in concerti:
Improvised cadenzas by the soloist.

Does the genre of concerto exist beyond the Classical Era?
Yes, it continues to be popular to the present day, although the form and structure become much less rigid, and the style changes in subsequent time periods.

FURTHER INVESTIGATION:

1. Listen to the exposition of a Classical concerto taking note of the first exposition being played by the orchestra and the repeat of the exposition featuring the soloist. Notice how even though the focus is different in each exposition, the thematic material is the same.
2. Listen to examples of concerti from the Baroque and Classical eras and compare the stylistic differences.

SUGGESTED LISTENING:

- Carl Stamitz's *Clarinet Concerto No. 3*
- Wolfgang Amadeus Mozart's *Piano Concerto No. 16*
- Franz Joseph Haydn's *Cello Concerto No. 2 in D major, Hob.VIIb:2*

Sonata

A **sonata** in the Classical Era is a multi-movement solo for piano OR a duo for piano and one other orchestral instrument. In these duo sonatas, the piano does not act as mere accompaniment but is an equal partner in the piece; both instruments have featured moments. As in the Baroque Era, the number of movements is flexible, although three movements is the norm. The titling of Classical Era sonatas can seem tricky to understand, but is easy to get used to once you understand the basics. If you see a title listed as simply

Sonata in B minor

you would have to guess as to whether it is a solo piano sonata or whether it also involves another instrument. If you see it titled as

Piano Sonata in B minor

you can be confident it is a solo piano sonata. If you see it titled as

Violin Sonata in B minor

you can be confident it is for violin and piano. When an orchestral instrument is listed before the word "sonata," the assumption is that a piano is also involved.

Performing forces for sonatas:
- solo instruments (piano sonatas were particularly popular)
- piano plus one orchestral instrument

Forms used in sonatas:
Any of the standard forms popular in the Classical Era, namely sonata form, variation form, minuet form, and rondo form. Keep in mind, if the sonata only has three movements, the minuet form is most likely to be excluded.

Does the genre of sonata exist beyond the Classical Era?
Yes, it continues to be popular to the present day, although the form and structure become much less rigid and the style changes in subsequent time periods.

Wolfgang Amadeus Mozart and his sister Nannerl at the keyboard, their father holding the violin. Copyright in the Public Domain.

FURTHER INVESTIGATION:

1. Listen to piano sonatas. Take note of how many movements there are and of which forms are used in each movement.
2. Listen to some sonatas for piano plus one other orchestral instrument and notice how the focus shifts constantly between the two instruments.
3. Listen to examples of sonatas from the Baroque *and* Classical eras and compare the stylistic differences.

SUGGESTED LISTENING:

- Wolfgang Amadeus Mozart's *Piano Sonata #5 in G, K 283*
- Franz Joseph Haydn's *Piano Sonata No. 60 in C major, Hob.XVI:50*
- Mozart's *Sonata in G for Oboe KV 379*
- Ludwig van Beethoven's *Horn Sonata in F major, Op. 17*

String Quartet

The **string quartet** is a chamber genre. The vast majority of string quartets are scored for two violins, one viola, and one cello; however, any combination of four string instruments can be considered a string quartet. String quartets generally have four movements. This genre came about as a result of the following:

1. Domestic performers wanted to perform symphonies in their homes but didn't have a full orchestra available to them. To make such performances possible, they reduced the usual required string performers to a single performer per part. Instead of six violins on the first violin part, there would only be one; instead of six violins on the second violin part, there would only be one; and so on.
2. The trio sonata of the Baroque Era featured two higher instruments and basso continuo (lower instrument plus keyboard). The string quartet may be a result of replacing the continuo players with viola and cello.
3. Some attribute the birth of string quartets to Haydn, because he standardized the structure and he wrote over sixty of them.

Forms used in the genre of string quartet:

The layout of a string quartet is extremely similar to the layout of the Classical symphony. Movement one is generally in sonata form; movement two is in whatever form the composer chooses, often variation form; movement three is in minuet form; and movement four is generally in rondo form (and occasionally sonata form or even the hybrid sonata-rondo form).

Franz Joseph Haydn playing with a string quartet.

Does the genre of string quartet exist beyond the Classical Era?

Yes, it continues to be popular to the present day, although the form and structure become much less rigid, and the style changes in subsequent time periods.

FURTHER INVESTIGATION:

1. Look up several Classical Era string quartets. Notice the layout of the movements and their similarities to the layouts of symphonies. Listen to one to see if the assumptions you made about which forms would be used are accurate.
2. Listen to string quartets by different Classical Era composers. See if you hear stylistic differences with each composer.

SUGGESTED LISTENING:

- Wolfgang Amadeus Mozart's *String Quartet No. 19 in C major, K. 465, "Dissonance"*
- Franz Joseph Haydn's *String Quartet No. 30 in E flat major, Op. 33, No. 2, Hob. III:38, "The Joke"*
- Ludwig van Beethoven's *String Quartet No. 3 in D major, Op. 18, No. 3*

Piano Trio

A **piano trio** is a multi-movement chamber work for piano and two other orchestral instruments, usually a violin and a cello. There is no set standard for how many movements are in a piano trio, but the majority of piano trios have three movements. This genre most likely developed as the keyboard part in a Baroque trio sonata became more than merely a continuo performer and began to take on a much more soloistic role.

Performing forces for piano trios:

Most commonly piano, violin and cello, but many composers wrote piano trios for other combinations such as piano, oboe, and bassoon or piano, clarinet, and cello. The only constant is the presence of the piano.

Forms used in piano trios:

Same as in Classical Era sonatas.

Does the genre of piano trio exist beyond the Classical Era?

Yes, it continues to be popular to the present day, although the form and structure become much less rigid, and the style changes in subsequent time periods.

FURTHER INVESTIGATION:

1. Listen to Classical Era piano trios. Take note of how many movements there are and of which forms are used in each movement.
2. Listen to Classical Era piano trios and notice how the focus passes from instrument to instrument.
3. Do a search online to see how many Classical Era piano trios you can find that feature the normal instrumentation of piano, violin, and cello. See how many you can find that feature different instrumentation.

SUGGESTED LISTENING:

- Wolfgang Amadeus Mozart's *Piano Trio No. 4 in E major, K. 542*
- Franz Joseph Haydn's *Keyboard Trio No. 16 in D major, Hob.XV:16*
- Ludwig van Beethoven's *Piano Trio No. 6 in E flat major, Op. 70, No. 2*

Wind Quintet

A **wind quintet** is a multi-movement chamber work for five wind instruments—flute, oboe, clarinet, bassoon, and horn. The standard number of movements in a Classical Era wind quintet is four, following the same structure as the symphony. The wind quintet was developed in part to showcase the principal (first chair) players of wind instruments in the Classical orchestra.

Forms used in wind quintets:
All the standard forms of the Classical Era are possible.

Does the genre of wind quintet exist beyond the Classical Era?
Yes, it continues to be popular to the present day, although the form and structure become much less rigid and the style changes in subsequent time periods.

FURTHER INVESTIGATION:

1. Listen to Classical Era wind quintets to determine which forms are being used in which movements.
2. Watch a performance of a Classical Era wind quintet to get to know the appearance and sound of this genre and its instruments.

- Franz Danzi's *Wind Quintet in G minor, Op. 56, No. 2*
- Antoine Reicha's *Wind Quintet No. 9 in D major, Op. 91, No. 3*
- Giuseppe Cambini's *Wind Quintet No. 3 in F major*

Other Chamber Music

There are as many combinations of instruments in the larger genre of chamber music as there are instruments in the orchestra. Because the string quartet is so popular during this time period, almost all chamber music in the Classical Era features string instruments. The titling of Classical Era chamber music can seem confusing at first, but is easy to get used to once you understand the basics. If you see a title listed thus,

> *Flute Trio in F Major*

you might assume that you will hear three flutists perform the piece. However, in the Classical Era, because string instruments were such a popular feature of chamber music, you should instead assume that you will hear flute plus two string instruments. This does not mean that the flute is more important than the other instruments, simply that the flute is the only non-string instrument involved in the piece. Similarly, if you see a title like this,

> *Piano Quartet in C# Minor*

you should assume that you will hear a piano and three strings perform the piece. If, on the other hand, the title does not specify a specific instrument, but instead highlights a family of instruments like so,

> *Woodwind Trio in A Minor*

there will be no strings involved at all.

Although there is not a standard number of movements in this vast array of combinations, three or four movements is common.

Performing forces for other chamber music in the Classical Era:
Varied, but generally grouped together in logical ways such as all strings, all woodwinds, or the specific genres with mixed instrumentation mentioned earlier (piano trio, sonatas, etc.).

FURTHER INVESTIGATION:

Enter random instruments and the words "Classical Era chamber music" into an online search to see the variety of combinations. Listen to them.

SUGGESTED LISTENING:

- Wolfgang Amadeus Mozart's *Serenade for Winds, K. 361*
- Mozart's *Clarinet Quintet in A major, K. 581*
- Carl Friedrich Abel's *Flute Quartet No. 1 in C major*

Opera

The definition of opera in the Classical Era is the same as it was in the Baroque Era. There are still operas categorized as opera seria and opera buffa. The types of musical numbers in opera are the same: recitative, aria, ensemble, and chorus numbers. The differences/new elements are as follows:

- Recitative is even *more* secco than before. This is also one of the few places in the Classical Era where you may still hear the harpsichord—as secco accompaniment in the recitative sections. Recitative in the Classical Era is much more conversational-sounding, and, therefore, more characteristic of actual human behavior.
- In the Baroque Era, ensemble numbers were practically synonymous with an aria but with two or three singers instead of a soloist. They were fairly static in terms of moving the plot forward. In the Classical Era, on the other hand, ensemble numbers
  - allow each performer to sing his/her own individual thoughts and feelings at the same time another character is singing about his/her individual thoughts and feelings
  - allow the emotions of the characters to change as the ensemble progresses
  - move the plot forward.

Mozart was particularly adept at using the ensemble number to move the plot forward and make the opera feel more natural and conversational. In his opera buffa, *The Marriage of Figaro*, there is a series of scenes that begins as a duo ensemble and ends with eight singers as part of the ensemble.

Performing forces for opera:
More than one singer (with orchestra).

Does the genre of opera exist beyond the Classical Era?
Yes. Opera continues to be a vital genre to the present day, but the style and structure has changed with each subsequent time period.

FURTHER INVESTIGATION:

1. Watch an entire Classical Era opera. Many online sources have complete operas available for viewing, but make certain that you pick an option that has subtitles so you know what is going on. Alternatively, if subtitles are not provided, you can acquire a libretto (with the original text and an English translation) to follow along with.
2. Watch at least a half hour (each) of an opera from the Classical Era and an opera from the Baroque Era to see how they differ in style, structure, and form.

SUGGESTED LISTENING:

- Wolfgang Amadeus Mozart's *The Marriage of Figaro*
- Mozart's *Cosi fan Tutte*
- Mozart's *Don Giovanni*

Singspiel

Singspiel is a type of German opera in which spoken dialogue takes the place of the typical recitative numbers. Most *singspiele* (plural) are comic in nature, but there are a few that feature more serious subjects. *Singspiele* still use aria, ensemble, and chorus numbers.

Does the genre of singspiel exist beyond the Classical Era?
Singspiele from the Classical Era are still performed regularly to the present day, but composers no longer write new *singspiele*, at least when it comes to art music.

Exceptions to the definition above:
If you search for *singspiel* on YouTube, the vast majority of the videos you will find are not art music; they are more akin to variety shows with vaudevillian comedy and sight gags. This is a pop version of singspiel in the folk tradition.

FURTHER INVESTIGATION:

Watch a Classical Era *singspiel* (with subtitles). Many online sources have complete *singspiele* available for viewing. You may need to search for "singspiel" along with a Classical Era composer's name to ensure you find one that is considered art music.

SUGGESTED LISTENING:

- Wolfgang Amadeus Mozart's *The Magic Flute*
- Mozart's *The Abduction from the Seraglio*
- *Mozart's Der Schauspieldirektor*

Mass

The Mass continues to be a vital music genre in the Classical Era. The only obvious change from Baroque to Classical is the style of music.

FURTHER INVESTIGATION:

Watch or listen to a Mass from the Classical Era, and then listen to one from an earlier time period. Note the differences in style and performing forces.

SUGGESTED LISTENING:

- Wolfgang Amadeus Mozart's *Requiem in D minor, K. 626*
- Franz Joseph Haydn's *Mass No. 13 in B flat major, Hob.XXII:13, "Creation Mass"*
- Ludwig van Beethoven's *Mass in D major, Op. 123, "Missa Solemnis"*

CHAPTER

FIFTEEN

Composers of the Classical Era

The three most celebrated composers of the Classical Era—Mozart, Haydn, and Beethoven—spent much of their careers in Vienna, Austria. They are known collectively as "The Vienna School."

Albrechtsberger, Johann Georg (1736-1809)

Country: Austria
Known for: Concerti
Recommended listening: *Concerto for Jaw Harp, Mandora and Orchestra in F Major*
("Jaw harp" is also referred to as "Jew's harp" in some publications/recordings)

Bach, Carl Philipp Emanuel (1714-1788)

Country: Germany
Known for: Symphonies
Recommended listening: *Sinfonia in F Major, Wq. 183/3*

Bach, Johann Christian (1735-1782)

Country: Germany
Known for: Concerti
Recommended listening: *Keyboard Concerto in E-Flat Major, Op. 7, No. 5, W. C59*

Bach, Johann Christoph Friedrich (1732-1795)

<u>Country:</u> Germany
<u>Known for:</u> Chamber music
<u>Recommended listening:</u> *Trio in C Major, W. VII/7*

Bach, Wilhelm Friedemann (1710-1784)

<u>Country:</u> Germany
<u>Known for:</u> Keyboard music
<u>Recommended listening:</u> *12 Polonaises, Fk. 12*

Ludwig van Beethoven
Copyright in the Public Domain.

Beethoven, Ludwig van (1770-1827)

- He was known for pushing the boundaries of what was acceptable in music form, structure, and tempo.
- He began to go deaf around the age of thirty—the condition made him contemplate suicide, but he felt there was too much music left in him to end his life.[1]
- Music critics generally criticized his music for breaking too many rules.[2] Performers complained that his music was too difficult and too fast.

<u>Country:</u> Germany
<u>Known for:</u> Symphonies
<u>Recommended listening:</u> *Triple Concerto for Violin, Cello and Piano in C major, Op. 56* especially the third movement.

Boccherini, Luigi (1743-1805)

<u>Country:</u> Italy
<u>Known for:</u> Chamber music
<u>Recommended listening:</u> *Guitar Quintet No. 7 in E Minor, G. 451*

---

1   William Kinderman, *Beethoven* (New York: Oxford, 2009), 69.
2   Piero Weiss and Richard Taruskin, eds., *Music in the Western World: A History in Documents* (New York: Schirmer, 1984), 328–329.

Boieldieu, François-Adrien (1775–1834)

Country: France
Known for: Opera
Recommended listening: *La dame blanche*

Cambini, Giuseppe Maria (1746–1825)

Country: Italy
Known for: Chamber music
Recommended listening: *Wind Quintet No. 2 in D Minor*

Cherubini, Luigi (1760–1842)

Country: Italy
Known for: Masses
Recommended listening: *Requiem No. 1 in C Minor*, especially the "Dies Irae"

Cimarosa, Domenico (1749–1801)

Country: Italy
Known for: Opera
Recommended listening: *Il matrimonio segreto*

Clementi, Muzio (1752–1832)

Country: England
Known for: Keyboard music
Recommended listening: *Piano Sonata in G Major, Op. 40, No. 1*

Cramer, Johann Baptist (1771–1858)

Country: Germany
Known for: Sonatas
Recommended listening: *Piano Sonata in D Major, Op. 25, No. 2*

Danzi, Franz (1763-1826)

<u>Country:</u> Germany
<u>Known for:</u> Chamber music
<u>Recommended listening:</u> *Wind Quintet in E Minor, Op. 67, No. 2*

Devienne, François (1759-1803)

<u>Country:</u> France
<u>Known for:</u> Flute music
<u>Recommended listening:</u> *Flute Concerto No. 9 in E Minor*

Dittersdorf, Carl Ditters von (1739-1799)

<u>Country:</u> Austria
<u>Known for:</u> Symphonies
<u>Recommended listening:</u> *Symphony No. 6 in A Major*

Dussek, Jan Ladislav (1760-1812)

<u>Country:</u> Czech Republic
<u>Known for:</u> Keyboard music
<u>Recommended listening:</u> *Piano Sonata in C Major, Op. 39, No. 2*

Fasch, Carl Friedrich Christian (1736-1800)

<u>Country:</u> Germany
<u>Known for:</u> Sacred music
<u>Recommended listening:</u> *Mass for sixteen voices*

Gossec, François-Joseph (1734-1829)

<u>Country:</u> Belgium
<u>Known for:</u> Symphonies
<u>Recommended listening:</u> *Symphony in B-Flat Major, Op. 6, No. 6*

Haydn, Franz Joseph (1732-1809)

- He worked for much of his career for the Ester-hazy family (Hungarian royalty).
- He wrote a number of compositions with formal titles followed by a nickname, provided either by his friends or by himself. For instance, the "Surprise," "Clock," "Drumroll," and "Farewell" symphonies, and the "Lark," "Joke," and "How Do You Do?" string quartets.[3]
- After his burial, his skull was stolen by a scientist interested in phrenology—the study of the bumps on the head as indication of skill and talent—not to be returned to the Austrian government until the 1950s.[4]

A bust of Franz Joseph Haydn

Country: Austria

Known for: Symphony

Recommended listening: *Symphony No. 45 in F sharp minor, Hob.I:45, "Farewell"* especially the first movement.

Haydn, Michael (1737-1806)

Country: Austria

Known for: Sacred music

Recommended listening: *Missa Sancti Hieronymi*

Hook, James (1746-1827)

Country: England

Known for: Art songs

Recommended listening: *Great Britain Triumphant*

---

3 Caryl Clark, *The Cambridge Companion to Haydn* (New York: Cambridge, 2005), 17–29.
4 R., "The Skull of Joseph Haydn," *The Musical Times* 73 (1932): 942–943.

Hummel, Johann Nepomuk (1778-1837)

<u>Country:</u> Austria
<u>Known for:</u> Concerto
<u>Recommended listening:</u> *Trumpet COncerto in E Major, WoO 1, S49*

Kreutzer, Rodolphe (1766-1831)

<u>Country:</u> France
<u>Known for:</u> Violin music
<u>Recommended listening:</u> *Violin Concerto No. 18 in E Minor*

Krommer, Franz (1759-1831)

<u>Country:</u> Czech Republic
<u>Known for:</u> Concerto
<u>Recommended listening:</u> *Concerto for 2 Clarinets in E-Flat Major, Op. 91*

Lebrun, Franziska (1756-1791)

<u>Country:</u> Germany
<u>Known for:</u> Sonata
<u>Recommended listening:</u> *Violin Sonata in F Major, Op. 1, No. 3*

Mozart, Wolfgang Amadeus (1756-1791)

- He was a child prodigy—along with his talented sister, he performed at courts all over Europe.[5]
- He wrote in both sacred and secular genres including over forty symphonies, over forty concerti, and a myriad of chamber music, solo piano music, and a number of highly influential operas.
- He is the subject of a movie (*Amadeus*) in which fellow composer Antonio Salieri is depicted as a villain partly responsible for Mozart's death. In real life, Salieri and Mozart were friendly, worked together on a cantata, and Salieri even taught music lessons to Mozart's son.[6]

---

5   Roye E. Wates, *Mozart: An Introduction to the Music, the Man, and the Myths* (Milwaukee: Amadeus, 2010), 54–55.
6   Jane Glover, *Mozart's Women: His Family, His Friends, His Music* (New York: Harper Collins, 2005), 334.

Country: Austria
Known for: Opera
Recommended listening: *The Marriage of Figaro*

Neukomm, Sigismund (1778-1858)

Country: Austria
Known for: Chamber music
Recommended listening: *Clarinet Quintet in B Major, Op. 8*

Paisiello, Giovanni (1740-1816)

Country: Italy
Known for: Opera
Recommended listening: *Il filosofi immaginari*

Pleyel, Ignaz (1757-1831)

Country: Austria
Known for: Chamber music
Recommended listening: *String Quartet in D Major, Op. 11, No. 3*

Reicha, Antonin (1770-1836)

Country: Czech Republic
Known for: Chamber music
Recommended listening: *Wind Quintet in D Minor, Op. 88, No. 4*

Salieri, Antonio (1750-1825)

Country: Italy
Known for: Opera
Recommended listening: *Der Rauchfangkehrer*

Soler, Vicente Martin y (1754-1806)

Country: Spain
Known for: Sonatas
Recommended listening: *Keyboard Sonata in D-Flat Major*

Sor, Fernando (1778-1839)

<u>Country:</u> Spain
<u>Known for:</u> Guitar music
<u>Recommended listening:</u> *Introduction and Variations on a theme by Mozart, Op. 9*

Stamitz, Carl (1745-1801)

<u>Country:</u> Germany
<u>Known for:</u> Concerto
<u>Recommended listening:</u> *Violin Concerto in C Major*

ROMANTIC ERA (1810-1910)

The Romantic Era is a time of great change in music, art, and literature. The forms and multi-movement genres, with their specific rules, are viewed as too restrictive and artificial. Form is not entirely abandoned, but genres with no set form become the norm. The absolute music of the past gives way to the program music of the Romantic Era. The art, music, and literature of the Romantic Era focuses more on human emotions than ever before.

Instruments in the Romantic Era

Woodwind, brass, string, and keyboard instruments continue to be used and perfected during the Romantic Era. The saxophone is invented in this time period. Even though the saxophone is made of metal, it is considered part of the woodwind family because it was invented by Adolphe Sax, who played both flute and clarinet and borrowed many design elements and mechanisms from each of those instruments.

Performance Venues in the Romantic Era

The church, court, opera house, concert hall, and private home continue to be important performance venues in the Romantic Era. With regard to chamber music, it becomes fashionable to invite performers and composers into your home for a private soirée with a group of invited friends. Many composers in the Romantic Era receive a fair amount of their financial support from wealthy people who want to be associated with them.

CHAPTER

SIXTEEN

Compositional and Performance Techniques, Forms, and Style Used in the Romantic Era

Forms: Strophic, Modified Strophic, and Through-Composed

These three forms are used in vocal music, particularly in the area of art songs.

Strophic form: Strophic form is when the same music is used for multiple verses of a song. For example, most hymns, patriotic songs, and children's songs are strophic—numerous verses, but the same music is used for each verse.

Modified strophic form: Modified strophic form is when the same music is used for MOST of the verses, but some verses are different or are altered to help further enhance the text.

Through-composed: It is actually a misnomer to refer to this as a form, because "through-composed" means that each verse has different music in an effort to enhance the text. In other words, there isn't really a structured form. There may be repetitive motives, but the exact music (per verse) is not repeated.

Genres that use these forms:
- Lieder
- Other art songs
- Some operatic arias

Are these forms used in music composed after the Romantic Era?
Yes.

FURTHER INVESTIGATION:

1. Listen to lots of Romantic Era art songs *with* the text (and translation) in front of you. Try to determine the form.
2. Listen to a Romantic Era song cycle to determine which songs within the song cycle are using which forms.

SUGGESTED LISTENING:

- Strophic form: Franz Schubert's *"Ungeduld"* from *Die schöne Mullerin*
- Modified strophic form: Schubert's *Gretchen am Spinnrade*
- Through-composed: Schubert's "Halt" from *Die schöne Mullerin*

Performance Technique: Rubato

This performance technique allows the performer to speed up or slow down the notes of a piece of music to enhance expressiveness. Certain notes can be stretched out and others can be shortened at the will of the performer. **Rubato** is not indicated in the score, with the exception of "tempo rubato" at the very beginning of the piece. Rubato is entirely up to the performer, which makes each performance unique.

Genres that use rubato:
- Any Romantic Era genre can use this technique.
- Most frequently used in character pieces and other solo pieces.

Is rubato used in music composed after the Romantic Era?
Yes, rubato continues to be a popular expressive technique in music.

FURTHER INVESTIGATION:

1. Listen to three different recordings of the exact same character piece from the Romantic Era. Notice how each performer utilizes rubato in his/her own way.
2. If capable, play a character piece on the piano (or find a piano-playing friend to do so) and try to figure out where your own emotions tell you to speed up or slow down.

SUGGESTED LISTENING:

- Frederic Chopin's *Prelude #7 in A major, Op. 28*
- Franz Liszt's "La chapelle de Guillaume Tell" from *Années de pèlerinage I, S.160*
- Edvard Grieg's "Illusion" from *Lyric Pieces, Book 6, Op. 57*

Compositional Technique: Leitmotiv

Leitmotivs are short melodies or fragments of melodies that represent people, places, objects, emotions, and intents. Leitmotivs are used in the music dramas of Richard Wagner. These short motives allow him to foreshadow events, alert the audience when a particular character is entering, or even express what a character is thinking about. It goes much deeper than that, however. Wagner wove these leitmotivs together in such intricacies that scholars today are still identifying (and debating) the hundreds of leitmotivs found in his music dramas.

Genres that use leitmotivs:
- Music dramas
- Symphonic poems
- Opera

Are leitmotivs used in music composed after the Romantic Era?
Yes, many composers of art music continue to use leitmotivs. In addition, film composers of today frequently use leitmotivs in film scores, especially in film series.

FURTHER INVESTIGATION:

1. Search online, using "leitmotiv" and "Wagner" as keywords. You will find lots of video explanations/examples of leitmotivs as well as articles and other links. Read/watch a few to better understand the influence of leitmotivs.
2. Search keywords "leitmotiv" and your favorite epic movie series (such as "Star Wars" or "Lord of the Rings"). You will discover that Wagner's technique of leitmotiv has become incredibly popular, especially in modern film music.

SUGGESTED LISTENING:

- Richard Wagner's *Der Ring des Nibelungen*
- Wagner's *Tristan und Isolde*
- Wagner's *Parsifal*

Compositional Technique: Idée Fixe

Similar to the leitmotiv, the **idée fixe** is a melody that represents a character in a story. Idée fixe literally means "fixed idea" or obsession. Unlike the short leitmotiv, the idée fixe is a relatively long melody and generally represents one thing within a larger work. It can change throughout a work to represent change within the character it represents. This term was used mainly by French composer Hector Berlioz. In his *Symphonie Fantastique* and *Lélio* (both large-scale symphonies), the idée fixe represents the main character's "beloved." In *Harold in Italy* (another symphony), the idée fixe represents the eponymous character.

Genres that feature the use of an idée fixe:
Berlioz is the only composer who used this particular term—idée fixe—but many composers were influenced by this use of recurring thematic material. It is possible that Wagner got his idea for leitmotivs after hearing the music of Berlioz.

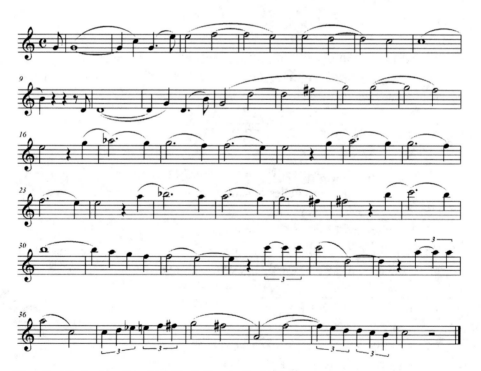

The entire idée fixe from *Symphonie Fantastique* by Hector Berlioz

FURTHER INVESTIGATION:

First, search online for "idée fixe from *Symphonie Fantastique*" and listen to it until you can hum it. Then listen to any part of Hector Berlioz's *Symphonie Fantastique*. Notice how many times it occurs within the symphony.

SUGGESTED LISTENING:

- Hector Berlioz's *Symphonie Fantastique*
- Berlioz's *Lélio*
- Berlioz's *Harold in Italy*

Style: Nationalism

Nationalism is a musical style in which the composer's nationality or homeland is reflected in some way within his/her music. This is done in a number of ways; the most common types of nationalistic music are as follows:

- Incorporating national folk tunes/dances/hymns within new compositions
- Composing arrangements of preexisting national tunes
- Composing programmatic works that describe some element of the composer's nationality or homeland
- Composing music intended to stir up patriotic feelings

There are not too many composers who are exclusively nationalistic, so it may be wiser to label individual pieces "nationalistic." Note: National anthems and patriotic songs (in most cases) are not considered to be art music.

Genres that feature Nationalism:
Any genre is possible.

Does the style of Nationalism exist after the Romantic Era?
Yes. Many composers incorporate nationalistic concepts into their compositions.

FURTHER INVESTIGATION:

1. Listen to recordings of nationalistic art music from one of the countries you have lived in or traveled to. Does the music remind you of that country?
2. Compare a piece of nationalistic art music from one country to a nationalistic piece of art music from another country. How are they different or similar?

3. Compose your own art music arrangement of a folk or dance tune from your homeland.

SUGGESTED LISTENING:

- Czech Republic
  - ○ Antonín Dvořák's *Slavonic Dance No. 10 in E minor, Op. 72, No. 2*
  - ○ Bedřich Smetana's *Má vlast*
- Finland:
  - ○ Jean Sibelius' *The Swan of Tuonela*
- Norway:
  - ○ Edvard Grieg's *Peer Gynt Suite No. 1, Op. 46*
- Poland:
  - ○ Any of Frédéric Chopin's "Polonaise" or "Mazurka" piano pieces.
- Russia:
  - ○ Mikhail Glinka's *Kamarinskaya*
  - ○ Modest Mussorgsky's *Night on the Bare Mountain*
  - ○ Alexander Borodin's *Prince Igor* (especially the Polovetsian Dances from Act II)
- Spain:
  - ○ Isaac Albéniz's *Iberia*
- United States:
  - ○ Anthony Philip Heinrich's *Barbecue Divertimento*
  - ○ Edward MacDowells' *New England Idyls, Op. 62*

CHAPTER

SEVENTEEN
Genres of the Romantic Era

Art Song

Art songs are songs for solo voice and piano meant to be performed in the comfort of one's living room. Operatic arias are not considered art songs, because they are not intended for voice and piano but for voice and orchestra. Art songs were popular throughout Europe and were written in whichever language the composer chose.

Forms used in art songs:
- Strophic form
- Modified strophic form
- Through-composed form

Does the genre of art songs exist beyond the Romantic Era?
Yes, art songs continue to be a vital genre to the present day.

FURTHER INVESTIGATION:

Listen to two or three Romantic Era art songs. Notice any similarities or differences in comparison with operatic arias.

SUGGESTED LISTENING:

- England
  - George Butterworth's *Six Songs from A Shropshire Lad*

- France
  - Emmanuel Chabrier's *L'invitation au voyage*
  - Pauline Viardot's *Les filles de Cadix*
- Italy
  - Vincenzo Bellini's *La Farfalletta*
  - Giuseppe Verdi's *Lo Spazzacamino*
- Norway:
  - Edvard Grieg's *Five Songs, Op. 69*
- United States:
  - Charles Griffes' *Three Poems of Fiona MacLeod, Op. 11*

Lied

A **lied** (plural: **lieder**) is an art song based on a German Romantic poem. The piano often acts as a programmatic partner with the voice in helping to tell the story.

Performing forces for lieder:
Solo voice and piano.

Forms used in lieder:
- Strophic form
- Modified strophic form
- Through-composed form

Exceptions to the definition above:
Sometimes composers would add an extra instrument to the voice and piano, such as the addition of a clarinet for Schubert's *Der Hirt auf dem Felsen*, but this is quite rare.

FURTHER INVESTIGATION:

Select some Romantic Era lieder. Read the text without listening to the music. Try to imagine what programmatic elements might be contributed by the piano. Then listen to the pieces to see if you were correct.

SUGGESTED LISTENING:

- Clara Schumann's *Liebst du um Schönheit*
- Robert Schumann's "Widmung" from *Myrthen, Op. 25*
- Franz Schubert's "Der Lindenbaum" from *Winterreise, Op. 89, D. 911*

Song Cycle

Many poets wrote collections of poetry in which all the poems shared a common theme. Romantic composers would take a collection of poetry as their text and compose an art song for each poem in the collection. This collection of art songs is known as a **song cycle**.

Performing forces for song cycles:
Solo voice and piano; solo voice and orchestra.

Does the genre of song cycle exist beyond the Romantic Era?
Yes, it continues to be a vital genre to the present day.

FURTHER INVESTIGATION:

Listen to a complete Romantic Era song cycle. Note the characteristics of this genre.

SUGGESTED LISTENING:

*   Gustav Mahler's *Kindertotenlieder*
*   Franz Schubert's *Winterreise*
*   Robert Schumann's *Dichterliebe*

Character Piece

A **character piece** is a relatively short solo piano piece with no set form. These are considered program music to a degree, although they are not necessarily meant to tell a story; in most cases, they are intended to convey, briefly, a particular emotion, mood, or character.

Titles of character pieces are varied. There are non-programmatic titles, somewhat programmatic titles, and completely programmatic titles.

Non-programmatic titles:
*   Bagatelle: Literally "a trifle"; a short, light-hearted piece—favored by Smetana and Sibelius
*   Capriccio: Literally "whim"; meant to sound as though the performers are making it up as they perform—favored by Brahms

- Étude: Literally "study"; term originated as short pieces intended to help an instrumentalist improve their performing technique—favored by Chopin and Liszt
- Humoresque: Term meant to evoke a good mood; "good humor"—favored by Dvořák
- Impromptu: Meant to evoke improvisation—favored by Schubert
- Intermezzo: Term originated as a short comic opera performed before a more serious opera—favored by Brahms
- Mazurka: Term originated as a Polish dance—favored by Chopin
- Moments musicaux: Literally "musical moments"—favored by Schubert
- Polonaise: Term originated as a Polish dance—favored by Chopin
- Rhapsody: A through-composed piece often incorporating nationalistic melodies—favored by Liszt
- Scherzo: Term originated with Beethoven, meaning "joke"; in the Romantic Era, scherzo means a fast, energetic piece—favored by Chopin
- Tarantella: Term originated as an Italian folk dance—used by many composers
- Waltz or Valse: Term originated as a triple meter dance from Germany—favored by Chopin

Somewhat programmatic titles:
- Ballade: Term originated as a poem about a hero, nature, or mythology—favored by many composers, including Chopin and Brahms
- Lied ohne Worte (Song without Words): Meant to emulate the human voice—favored by Mendelssohn
- Lyric piece: Meant to evoke a short poem—exclusively used by Grieg
- Nocturne: Literally means "of the night"; generally a dream-like piece—favored by Field and Chopin
- Novelette: Term meant to emulate a romantic story—favored (invented) by Robert Schumann
- Prelude: Term originally referred to a piece that occurred before another piece of music and was often paired (*Prelude and Fugue*, for example, in the Baroque Era); in the Romantic Era, it is meant to evoke a brief glimpse of an emotion or mood—favored by Chopin

Programmatic titles:
Because programmatic titles are descriptive, the possibilities of titles for programmatic character pieces are endless. Here are some examples of actual titles (translated) of character pieces by a few composers:

Franz Liszt

- *The Thinker*
- *Marriage of the Virgin*
- *The Fountains of the Villa d'Este*
- *The Mournful Gondola*

Robert Schumann

- *Soaring*
- *Why?*
- *In the Night*
- *Butterflies*

Edvard Grieg

- *The Pig*
- *Wedding Day at Troldhaugen*
- *I Wander Deep in Thought*
- *Have You by Chance Seen My Wife?*

Performing forces for character pieces:

Solo piano

Performance techniques used in character pieces:

Rubato

Does the genre of the character piece exist beyond the Romantic Era?

Yes, it continued to be a vital genre well into the Twentieth Century.

Exceptions to the definition above:

Some composers wrote character pieces for piano and one other orchestral instrument, but these are considerably less common than the solo piano character pieces.

FURTHER INVESTIGATION:

Listen to various types of Romantic Era character pieces. Notice the varieties and the use of rubato.

SUGGESTED LISTENING:

- Frédéric Chopin's *24 Preludes, Op. 28*
- Johannes Brahms' *3 Intermezzos, Op. 117*
- Felix Mendelssohn's *Lieder ohne Worte (Songs without Words), Book 2, Op. 30*

Program Symphony

The genre of the symphony, as it existed in the Classical Era, continues to be popular well into the Romantic Era. Many Romantic Era composers write symphonies using the same four-movement structure and same forms as the symphonies of the Classical Era. But another type of symphony evolved in the Romantic Era, known as the **program symphony**. Program symphonies tell a story using program music. There are no limitations as to number of movements or which forms (if any) are used. In many cases, when these are performed, the composer provides the written storyline (known as the "program" of the piece) in the printed program. Audiences would read the program beforehand so they could follow along with the programmatic telling of the story.

Performing forces for program symphonies:
Romantic Era orchestra. The instrumentation for program symphonies is expanded considerably; composers introduce more instruments to the orchestra than normal—new instruments, vocalists, narration, etc.

Does the genre of program symphony exist beyond the Romantic Era?
Yes, but very few composers refer to it as such.

Exceptions to the definition above:
There are examples of Romantic Era large-scale orchestral works that appear to be program symphonies but are given a different name by the composer—for example, "Symphonic Suite" or "Symphonic Poem."

FURTHER INVESTIGATION:

1. Listen to a complete Romantic Era program symphony. Obtain the written program so you can read the storyline as you listen.
2. Watch or listen to at least a half hour (each) of a Romantic Era symphony and a Classical Era symphony. Note the stylistic differences.

SUGGESTED LISTENING:

- Felix Mendelssohn's *Symphony No. 3, "Scottish"*
- Hector Berlioz's *Symphonie Fantastique*
- Franz Liszt's *Faust Symphony*

Concert Overture

A **concert overture** is a single-movement orchestral piece. It is not a traditional overture (at the start of an opera, oratorio, or suite); instead, it is one piece among many pieces in a concert. Near the start of the Romantic Era, orchestras had taken to playing the overtures of popular operas or oratorios in concerts. After a while, composers of the Romantic Era decided to write overtures that weren't even attached to a larger work. Concert overtures are generally programmatic in nature.

Performing forces used in concert overtures:
Romantic Era orchestra.

Forms used in concert overtures:
Sonata form was used early on, but as time progressed, composers quit using forms and concert overtures became less restrictive.

Does the genre of concert overture exist beyond the Romantic Era?
Yes, but not as common as in the Romantic Era.

FURTHER INVESTIGATION:

Listen to at least two complete Romantic Era concert overtures. Note the characteristics of this genre.

SUGGESTED LISTENING:

- Felix Mendelssohn's *Hebrides Overture "Fingal's Cave"*
- Hector Berlioz's *Rob Roy Overture*
- Pyotr Ilyich Tchaikovsky's *1812 Overture*

Symphonic Poem/Tone Poem

A single-movement work for orchestra. This genre evolved from the "concert overture." **Symphonic poems** and **tone poems** rarely follow any set form—they are instead free-flowing in order to tell a story (program music).

Performing forces used in symphonic poems/tone poems:
Romantic Era orchestra.

Does the genre of symphonic poem/tone poem exist beyond the Romantic Era?
Yes, it particularly flourished in the first half of the Twentieth Century.

Exceptions to the definition above:
Every composer seemed to like to label his/her orchestral works with a unique genre, so a lot of pieces that fit the definition of symphonic poem/tone poem are referred to by varied labels, such as "poematic symphony" or "fantasy-overture." Some composers wrote multi-movement works (program symphony), or compositions featuring a solo instrument with orchestra (concerto), yet referred to them as symphonic poems or tone poems.

FURTHER INVESTIGATION:

Listen to a complete Romantic Era symphonic poem/tone poem. Note the characteristics of this genre.

SUGGESTED LISTENING:

* Bedřich Smetana's *Má vlast*
* Franz Liszt's *Mazeppa*
* Camille Saint-Saëns' *Danse macabre*
* César Franck's *Les Djinns*

Opera

The definition of opera in the Romantic Era is the same as in previous time periods, but there are a few changes. Although there is still the use of recitative, aria, ensemble, and chorus, everything leans much more toward ensemble. It often seems as though Romantic Era operas are one really long ensemble number. This is a positive thing when it comes to realism. Even though opera by its very definition (a story told entirely through acting and singing) is not exactly realistic, the Romantic composers tried to achieve more realism by attempting to avoid the problems of earlier time periods. The main challenge to realism previously was the fact that every so often the action would come to a standstill while someone sang an aria or when a chorus occurred. In Romantic operas, even if there is an aria, it generally occurs in a much more realistic way—in most cases, 1) the action doesn't stop, 2) the person isn't necessarily singing an inner monologue, 3) other characters are more involved in hearing the aria and reacting to it, and 4) most arias turn into an ensemble number as other characters react to whatever emotion or concept the soloist is singing about.

<u>**Performing forces for Romantic Era opera:**</u>
Romantic orchestra and singers.

<u>**Does the genre of opera exist beyond the Romantic Era?**</u>
Yes, opera continues to be a vital genre to the present day, although the style changes with each new time period.

FURTHER INVESTIGATION:

1. Watch an entire Romantic Era opera. Many online sources have complete operas available for viewing, but make certain that you pick an option that has subtitles so you know what is going on. Alternatively, if subtitles are not provided, you can acquire a libretto (with the original text and an English translation) with which to follow along.
2. Watch at least a half hour (each) of an opera from the Romantic Era and an opera from an earlier time period to see how they differ in style, structure, and form.
3. Listen to or watch a Romantic opera. Note the differences between Romantic opera and Classical opera.

SUGGESTED LISTENING:

*   Giuseppe Verdi's *Aida*
*   Gaetano Donizetti's *Lucia di Lammermoor*
*   Vincenzo Bellini's *Norma*

Music Drama/Gesamtkunstwerk

Music Drama, or **Gesamtkunstwerk** (literally "Total Work of Art"), is what German composer Richard Wagner called his own operas. Despite Romantic efforts to make opera more realistic, Wagner felt that most Romantic operas had not achieved a convincing level of realism. His attempts to separate himself from other opera composers led him to coin these new terms for his own operas. He preferred these terms instead of "opera" because he was striving for a new kind of opera in which the orchestra helped express emotion more directly than mere words can achieve.

He attempted this in a few different ways:

*   His groundbreaking use of leitmotivs, which help the audience make connections to individual characters more immediately, whether that character is on stage or not.

- The use of what he called "unending melody." The melodies in Wagner's music dramas go on and on, rarely reaching a solid cadence point. This is much more true to real human emotion—not contained in neat, evenly-spaced packages, but evolving and developing as each moment passes.
- His own libretti. Wagner is one of the only opera composers in all of music history to act as his own librettist. He felt that in order to create a perfect opera, the same creative force must be in control of both the music and the words. As a side note, he also influenced the sets, staging, and costuming; he wrote lengthy texts on the philosophy behind his music dramas; and he even designed an opera house that was built to his specifications.

Performing forces for music drama:
Romantic orchestra (with a much-expanded brass section) and singers.

Compositional techniques used in music drama:
Leitmotivs.

Does the genre of music drama exist beyond the Romantic Era?
Despite the continued popularity of Wagner's music dramas (they continue to be performed at opera houses throughout the world), other composers did not use the term.

Set design for the second music drama in Wagner's Ring Cycle, *Die Walküre*.

Exceptions to the definition above:
Not all of Wagner's operas were referred to as "music drama," nor did they all use leitmotivs. He wrote a lot of operas before he started using leitmotivs.

FURTHER INVESTIGATION:

Watch a performance of one of Wagner's music dramas. Note the characteristics unique to music drama.

SUGGESTED LISTENING:

- Richard Wagner's *Der Ring des Nibelungen* (this is a cycle of four operas)
    - *Das Rheingold*
    - *Die Walküre*
    - *Siegfried*
    - *Götterdämmerung*

French Grand Opera

A type of opera (in the French language) in which everything is grand—the length, the cast, and the spectacle.

Length: **French Grand Operas** generally have five acts, as opposed to the normal three (or, at the most, four) found in Italian and German operas. Because intermissions occur between each act (presuming that an intermission lasts for fifteen minutes—a conservative length), attending a French Grand Opera is a real commitment.

Cast: Many of these operas feature more than the normal number of leading characters. Traditional operas have one male and one female lead, maybe two of each, but French Grand Operas have numerous main characters, a very large chorus, and dancers.

Spectacle: Because a lot of French Grand Operas are based on historical events, set designers go to great lengths to re-create historic sites and architecture on stage. Also, the special effects are elaborate, including re-creations of massacres, volcanoes, executions, and ghostly visitations.

Performing forces for French Grand Opera:
Massive orchestras and large numbers of singers.

Does the genre of French Grand Opera exist beyond the Romantic Era?
Although no one composes French Grand Operas any more, they are still performed in opera houses all over the world. Unfortunately, because of the cost of producing

these operas (set design, large casts) they are performed far less frequently than they deserve and most often in truncated form.

FURTHER INVESTIGATION:

1. Search for articles/books about the genre of French Grand Opera and read descriptions of the size and scale of these massive works.
2. Watch a Romantic Era French Grand Opera performance. Note the characteristics unique to French Grand Opera.

SUGGESTED LISTENING:

- Giacomo Meyerbeer's *Robert le Diable*
- Meyerbeer's *Les Huguenots*
- Meyerbeer's *Le prophète*

Verismo

Verismo (translated as "realism") was a term to describe Italian operas in which humanity was depicted in a realistic way, often focusing on the lower classes, infidelity, and death.

Performing forces for verismo opera:
Romantic orchestra and singers.

Does the genre of verismo opera exist beyond the Romantic Era?
Although no one composes verismo operas any more, they are still performed in opera houses all over the world.

Exceptions to the definition above:
There is some disagreement as to which operas qualify as verismo. For instance, George Bizet's *Carmen*, which was all about the lower classes, infidelity, and death, is often excluded from this definition because it is in French, not Italian.

FURTHER INVESTIGATION:

Watch a complete Romantic Era verismo opera performance. Note how the subject matter is different from other types of opera in this and earlier time periods.

SUGGESTED LISTENING:

- Pietro Mascagni's *Cavalleria rusticana*
- Ruggero Leoncavallo's *Pagliacci*
- Giacomo Puccini's *Il tabarro*

Paraphrase/Transcription/Arrangement

Paraphrase, **transcription**, and **arrangement** are rewrites of preexisting compositions for a different instrument or ensemble. This is an opportunity for the composer to show his/her ability to create a new, and sometimes improved, version of a preexisting piece.

Paraphrase: When a composer takes a preexisting piece of music and rewrites it with considerable new material added (extra notes, new rhythms, new harmonies, etc.).

Transcription: When a composer takes a preexisting piece and re-writes it changing *only* the performing forces—same piece, different instrumentation—for example, taking an operatic aria and re-writing it (transcribing it) for wind ensemble.

Arrangement: When a composer takes a piece of music and rewrites it by changing the *style* of the piece considerably—for instance, taking a Classical Era string quartet and rewriting it (arranging it) in a rock-and-roll style.

Performing forces for paraphrase/transcription/arrangement:
As varied as the instruments and voices available.

FURTHER INVESTIGATION:

1. Find a Romantic Era paraphrase. First, listen to the piece upon which the paraphrase is based. Then listen to the paraphrase to see how much or how little it has been changed.
2. Find a Romantic Era transcription. First, listen to the piece upon which the transcription is based. Then listen to the transcription to see how it is literally exactly the same piece—only the instrumentation has changed.

SUGGESTED LISTENING:

- Paraphrase
  - Franz Liszt's *Rigoletto Paraphrase de Concert, S.434*
  - William Vincent Wallace's *Fantaisie brillante sur des motifs de l'opera La Traviata de Verdi, Op. 63*
  - Hugo Wolf's *Paraphrase uber Die Walkure von Richard Wagner*

- Transcription
  - Franz Liszt's *Grandes études d'après les caprices de Paganini*—originally composed by Niccolò Paganini for solo violin, transcribed by Liszt for piano.
  - Sigismond Thalberg's *The Art of Singing Applied to the Piano, Op.70, #5: Lacrimosa from Requiem by Mozart*—originally composed by Wolfgang Amadeus Mozart for orchestra and choir, transcribed by Thalberg for piano.
  - Max Reger's *Brandenburg Concerto No. 2 in F major*—originally composed by Johann Sebastian Bach for orchestra and soloists, transcribed by Reger for piano.
  - Ludwig van Beethoven's *Symphony No. 2*—originally composed by Beethoven for orchestra, transcribed by Beethoven himself for piano trio (violin, cello, piano).

A scene from Tchaikovsky's ballet *The Nutcracker.*

Ballet

Ballet is a genre in which a story is told (and depicted) wordlessly through music and dance. Although its roots are in earlier time periods, some of the most-performed ballets of all time are from the Romantic Era. Even though this is a largely visual art form, it is considered important in music history and literature because the music plays such a large programmatic role in the performance.

Performing forces for ballet:
Pit orchestra and dancers.

Does the genre of ballet exist beyond the Romantic Era?
Yes, ballet continues to be a vital genre to the present day.

FURTHER INVESTIGATION:

1. Watch a complete Romantic Era ballet performance. Note how much the orchestra helps in telling the story (through programmatic means).
2. Watch or listen to a Romantic Era ballet and a ballet from an earlier time period. Note the stylistic differences.

SUGGESTED LISTENING:

- Leo Delibes' *Coppélia*
- Pyotr Ilyich Tchaikovsky's *Swan Lake*, *Sleeping Beauty*, and *The Nutcracker*
- Adolphe Adam's *Giselle*

Concerto

The genre of Concerto continues to be popular in the Romantic Era. The only differences from previous time periods are

- Less reliance on form
- Less strictness with the number of movements
- Cadenzas written out by the composer, as opposed to the improvised cadenzas of previous time periods

Performing forces for concerti:
Solo instrument plus Romantic orchestra.

Does the genre of concerto exist beyond the Romantic Era?
Yes, it continues to be popular to the present day, but the style changes with each new time period.

FURTHER INVESTIGATION:

1. Watch or listen to a concerto composed in the Romantic Era.
2. Obtain a score to a Romantic Era concerto and look at the cadenza to see that it is completely written out by the composer—no improvisation.
3. Watch or listen to a Romantic Era concerto and a concerto from an earlier time period. Note the stylistic differences.

SUGGESTED LISTENING:

- Frédéric Chopin's *Piano Concerto No. 2 in F minor, Op. 21*
- Franz Liszt's *Piano Concerto No. 2 in A major, S125/R456*
- Pyotr Ilyich Tchaikovsky's *Violin Concerto in D major, Op. 35*
- Antonín Dvořák's *Cello Concerto in B minor, Op. 104, B. 191*

Chamber Music

The definition of chamber music, and the manner in which its various types are labeled (string quartet, piano trio, etc.) is the same as in the Classical Era. The main difference in the Romantic Era is the freedom from form and structure. As mentioned earlier, it was fashionable to host chamber music performances in your home. The composer, Franz Liszt, however, moved solo piano music from the chamber to the concert hall because he wanted larger audiences for his music. Other composers and performers liked the idea, and a large variety of chamber music began to be performed in concert halls.

Performing forces for chamber music:
Same as in the Classical Era—string quartet, wind quintet, piano trio, etc. A few combinations came to the forefront in the Romantic Era, particularly the piano quintet (one piano, four string instruments).

Does the genre of chamber music exist beyond the Romantic Era?
Yes, it continues to be popular to the present day, but the style changes with each new time period.

FURTHER INVESTIGATION:

1. Enter random instruments and the words "Romantic Era chamber music" into an online search to see the variety of combinations. Listen to them.
2. Watch or listen to some Romantic Era chamber music and some chamber music from an earlier time period. Note the stylistic differences.

SUGGESTED LISTENING:

- Robert Schumann's *Piano Quintet in E flat major, Op. 44*
- Franz Schubert's *Piano Quintet in A major, D. 667, "Trout"*
- Johannes Brahms' *Piano Quintet in F minor, Op. 34*

Sonata

The sonata continues to be a popular genre for composers and performers. The definition stays the same—a multi-movement solo for piano OR duo for piano and one other orchestral instrument. Unlike in the Classical Era, the number of movements is extremely flexible, and the reliance on form is minimized.

FURTHER INVESTIGATION:

1. Watch or listen to a sonata composed in the Romantic Era.
2. Watch or listen to a Romantic Era sonata and a sonata from an earlier time period. Note the stylistic differences.

SUGGESTED LISTENING:

- Franz Liszt's *Piano Sonata in B minor, S.178*
- Frédéric Chopin's *Piano Sonata No. 2 in B-flat minor, Op. 35*
- Edvard Grieg's *Sonata in A minor for cello and piano, Op. 36*
- Johannes Brahms' *Violin Sonata No. 3 in D minor, Op. 108*

Mass

The biggest change to the genre of the Mass in the Romantic Era is the performance purpose. Many Masses were still written specifically for church services, but a lot of composers wrote Masses to be performed as concert pieces.

FURTHER INVESTIGATION:

1. Watch or listen to a Mass composed in the Romantic Era.
2. Watch or listen to at least a half hour (each) of a Romantic Era Mass and a Mass from an earlier time period. Note the stylistic differences.

SUGGESTED LISTENING:

- Anton Bruckner's *Mass No. 1 in D minor, WAB 26*
- Gioachino Rossini's *Petite messe solennelle*
- Giuseppe Verdi's *Messa da Requiem*

CHAPTER EIGHTEEN
Composers of the Romantic Era

Adam, Adolphe (1803-1856)

<u>Country:</u> France
<u>Known for:</u> Opera
<u>Recommended listening:</u> *Giselle* (ballet)

Albéniz, Isaac (1860-1909)

<u>Country:</u> Spain
<u>Known for:</u> Piano works
<u>Recommended listening:</u> *Iberia, Book 2*

Auber, Daniel- François-Esprit (1782-1871)

<u>Country:</u> France
<u>Known for:</u> Opera
<u>Recommended listening:</u> *Fra Diavolo, S. 18*

Balakirev, Mily (1837-1910)

<u>Country:</u> Russia
<u>Known for:</u> Nationalistic music
<u>Recommended listening:</u> *Islamey*

Bellini, Vincenzo (1801-1835)

<u>Country:</u> Italy
<u>Known for:</u> Opera
<u>Recommended listening:</u> *Norma*

Berlioz, Hector (1803-1869)

Hector Berlioz
Copyright in the Public Domain

- Fell in love with an actress named Harriet Smithson. He became obsessed with her and stalked her for a time. He wrote a program symphony—*Symphonie Fantastique*—inspired by his obsession with Harriet. As a result, a few years later, Harriet Smithson married him.[1]
- In his sixties, after his first and second wives had passed away, he pursued a relationship with a woman he had first fallen in love with when he was a child and she was a teenager. She told him that he was absurd and that they hardly knew each other, but she agreed to one letter a year and one visit a year. They became close friends and regular pen pals for the remainder of their lives.[2]

<u>Country:</u> France
<u>Known for:</u> Program symphony
<u>Recommended listening:</u> *Tristia, Op. 18* especially the third movement

Bizet, Georges (1838-1875)

- When he composed the famous "Habanera" for his opera *Carmen,* he thought he had based it on an anonymously composed folk song. After the opera was performed for the first time, Bizet discovered that the melody was actually written by a known composer, Sebastián Iradier, and he added an attribution to the published score.[3]

<u>Country:</u> France
<u>Known for:</u> Opera
<u>Recommended listening:</u> *Carmen*

---

1 Henry Wall, "Habeneck and His Snuff-box," *The Musical Times* 78 (1937): 638.
2 D. Kern Holoman, *Berlioz* (Cambridge: Harvard, 1989), 574–585.
3 Susan McClary, *Georges Bizet: Carmen* (New York: Cambridge 1992), 51–52.

Scene from Bizet's opera *Carmen*

Boiti, Arrigo (1842-1918)

<u>Country:</u> Italy
<u>Known for:</u> Opera
<u>Recommended listening:</u> *Mefistofele*

Borodin, Alexander (1833-1887)

<u>Country:</u> Russia
<u>Known for:</u> Opera
<u>Recommended listening:</u> *Prince Igor*

Bottesini, Giovanni (1821-1889)

<u>Country:</u> Italy
<u>Known for:</u> Double-bass virtuoso pieces
<u>Recommended listening:</u> *Gran duo concertante*

Johannes Brahms

Brahms, Johannes (1833-1897)

- As a young teen, he made money by playing piano in bars.[4]
- He preferred to use Classical Era structure and form.
- He used metric displacement to make music in one meter sound as though it were in another meter for relatively short sections within a piece.

Country: Germany
Known for: Chamber music
Recommended listening: *Piano Quintet in F minor, Op. 34,* especially the third movement

Bruch, Max (1838-1920)

Country: Germany
Known for: Orchestral works
Recommended listening: *Violin Concerto No. 1 in G Minor, Op. 26*

Bruckner, Anton (1824-1896)

Country: Austria
Known for: Symphony
Recommended listening: *Symphony No. 9 in D Minor, WAB 109*

Busoni, Ferruccio (1866-1924)

Country: Italy
Known for: Piano Music
Recommended listening: *Piano Concerto, Op. 39*

Chabrier, Emmanuel (1841-1894)

Country: France
Known for: Opera
Recommended listening: *Le roi malgré lui*

---

4   Jan Swafford, *Johannes Brahms: A Biography* (New York: Random House, 1997), 28–30.

Crusell, Bernhard Henrik (1775-1838)

<u>Country:</u> Finland
<u>Known for:</u> Concerto
<u>Recommended listening:</u> *Clarinet Concerto No. 3 in B-Flat Major, Op. 11*

Chopin, Frédéric (1810-1849)

Frédéric Chopin near the end of his life.
Copyright in the Public Domain.

- He was plagued with a persistent cough throughout his life.
- During a revolution in Poland, his friends encouraged him to move away; they feared he was too weak to survive otherwise. He moved to Paris, but honored his homeland with many nationalistic compositions evoking dances and folk tunes of his native land.
- He had a lengthy relationship with Aurora Dudevant (an author with the pen name of George Sand). Their relationship ended after she wrote a novel—*Lucrezia Floriani*—that struck a little too close to home; it was about a woman who unhappily took care of a sickly man.[5]

<u>Country:</u> Poland
<u>Known for:</u> Character pieces
<u>Recommended listening:</u> *24 Preludes, Op. 28*

Cui, César (1835-1918)

<u>Country:</u> Russia
<u>Known for:</u> Art songs
<u>Recommended listening:</u> *7 Poems, Op. 33*

Czerny, Carl (1791-1857)

<u>Country:</u> Austria
<u>Known for:</u> Keyboard music

---

5 Tad Szulc, *Chopin in Paris: The Life and Times of the Romantic Composer* (New York: Scribner, 1998), 357.

<u>Recommended listening</u>: *Introduction, Variations et Polonaise sur Tu Vedrai la Sventurata dans Il Pirata de Bellini, Op. 160*

Delibes, Léo (1836–1891)

<u>Country</u>: France
<u>Known for</u>: Opera
<u>Recommended listening</u>: *Lakmé*

Donizetti, Gaetano (1797–1848)

<u>Country</u>: Italy
<u>Known for</u>: Opera
<u>Recommended listening</u>: *Lucia di Lammermoor*

Dukas, Paul (1865–1935)

<u>Country</u>: France
<u>Known for</u>: Orchestral music
<u>Recommended listening</u>: *The Sorceror's Apprentice*

Duparc, Henri (1848–1933)

<u>Country</u>: France
<u>Known for</u>: Art songs
<u>Recommended listening</u>: *La vie antérieure*

Dvořák, Antonín (1841–1904)

<u>Country</u>: Czech Republic
<u>Known for</u>: Symphony
<u>Recommended listening</u>: *Symphony No. 9 in E Minor, Op. 95, B. 178 "From the New World"*

Elgar, Edward (1857–1934)

<u>Country</u>: England
<u>Known for</u>: Orchestral music
<u>Recommended listening</u>: *Variations on an Original Theme, Op. 36 "Enigma"*

Erkel, Ferenc (1810-1893)

Country: Hungary
Known for: Opera
Recommended listening: *Bánk bán*

Fauré, Gabriel (1845-1924)

Country: France
Known for: Art songs
Recommended listening: *La bonne Chanson, Op. 61*

Field, John (1782-1837)

Country: Ireland
Known for: Character pieces
Recommended listening: *Nocturne No. 5 in B-Flat Major, H. 37A*

Franck, César (1822-1890)

Country: Belgium
Known for: Orchestral music
Recommended listening: *Symphony in D Minor*

Gade, Niels (1817-1890)

Country: Denmark
Known for: Choral music
Recommended listening: *Baldur's Dream, Op. 117*

Glazunov, Alexander (1865-1936)

Country: Russia
Known for: Orchestral music
Recommended listening: *Raymonda, Op. 57* (ballet)

Glinka, Mikhail (1804-1857)

Country: Russia

Known for: Orchestral music
Recommended listening: *Ruslan and Ludmilla (Overture)*

Gottschalk, Louis Moreau (1829-1869)

Country: USA
Known for: Piano Music
Recommended listening: *Souvenir de la Havane, Op. 39*

Gounod, Charles (1818-1893)

Country: France
Known for: Opera
Recommended listening: *Romeo et Juliette*

Grieg, Edvard (1843-1907)

Country: Norway
Known for: Character pieces
Recommended listening: *Wedding Day at Troldhaugen, Op. 65*

Holst, Gustav (1874-1934)

Country: England
Known for: Orchestral suite
Recommended listening: *The Planets, Op. 32*

Humperdinck, Engelbert (1854-1921)

Country: Germany
Known for: Opera
Recommended listening: *Hansel and Gretel*

Indy, Vincent d' (1851-1931)

Country: France
Known for: Orchestral music
Recommended listening: *Symphonie sur un chant montagnard francais, Op. 25*

Lalo, Édouard (1823-1892)

Country: France
Known for: Orchestral music
Recommended listening: *Symphonie Espagnole in D Minor, Op. 21* (violin concerto)

Leoncavallo, Ruggero (1857-1919)

Country: Italy
Known for: Verismo opera
Recommended listening: *Pagliacci*

Liszt, Franz (1811-1886)

- A virtuoso pianist who toured extensively, Liszt had rabid fans who would gather outside his hotel calling his name. He had many affairs, including some scandalous ones with the Countess Marie d'Agoult (she later became an author under the pen name of Daniel Stern) and the Princess Carolyn Sayn-Wittgenstein (also an author).[6]
- In his later years, he settled down and took holy orders and was known as Abbé (a religious title) Liszt.

Country: Hungary
Known for: Character pieces
Recommended listening: *Der Tanz in der Dorfschenke, S514/R181, "Mephisto Waltz No. 1"*

Franz Liszt

MacDowell, Edward (1860-1908)

Country: USA
Known for: Character pieces
Recommended listening: *Woodland Sketches, Op. 51*

---

6 Christopher H. Gibbs and Dana Gooley, eds. *Franz Liszt and His World* (Princeton: Princeton, 2006), 538–539.

Gustav Mahler's composition hut at Steinbach-am-Attersee.

Mahler, Gustav (1860-1911)

• While conductor at the Vienna State Opera House, he established new etiquette "rules" for art music audiences, including silence between movements, a rule that has remained in force to this day.

• He preferred to spend his summers in the countryside or mountains composing music in a small hut with nature surrounding him to inspire him.[7]

<u>Country:</u> Austria
<u>Known for:</u> Symphony
<u>Recommended listening:</u> *Symphony No. 2 in C minor, "Resurrection"*

Mascagni, Pietro (1863-1945)

<u>Country:</u> Italy
<u>Known for:</u> Verismo opera
<u>Recommended listening:</u> *Cavalleria Rusticana*

Massenet, Jules (1842-1912)

<u>Country:</u> France
<u>Known for:</u> Opera
<u>Recommended listening:</u> *Thaïs*

Mendelssohn, Fanny (1805-1847)

<u>Country:</u> Germany
<u>Known for:</u> Piano music
<u>Recommended listening:</u> *Piano Sonata in G Minor*

---

7   Norman Lebrecht, *Why Mahler?: How One Man and Ten Symphonies Changed Our World* (New York: Random House, 2010), 62.

Mendelssohn, Felix (1809–1847)

- He composed a number of programmatic works that evoked images of various countries. Among the most famous of these are *Hebrides Overture, "Fingal's Cave,"* about the island of Staffa off the west coast of Scotland, and his *Symphony #3, "Scottish,"* and *Symphony #4, "Italian."*
- When he received the news that his sister had died unexpectedly, he collapsed of shock and struck his head. He never recovered and died later that same year.[8]

Country: Germany
Known for: Orchestral music
Recommended listening: *A Midsummer Night's Dream, Op. 61*

Meyerbeer, Giacomo (1791–1864)

Country: Germany
Known for: French Grand Opera
Recommended listening: *Les Huguenots*

Mussorgsky, Modest (1839–1881)

Country: Russia
Known for: Orchestral program music
Recommended listening: *Night on Bald Mountain*

Offenbach, Jacques (1819–1880)

Country: France
Known for: Opera
Recommended listening: *The Tales of Hoffmann*

Paganini, Niccolò (1782–1840)

Country: Italy
Known for: Violin music
Recommended listening: *24 Caprices for Solo Violin, Op. 1*

---

8   R. Larry Todd, *Mendelssohn: A Life in Music* (New York: Oxford, 2003), 557.

Puccini, Giacomo (1858-1924)

Country: Italy
Known for: Verismo opera
Recommended listening: *La bohème*

Rimsky-Korsakov, Nikolai (1844-1908)

Country: Russia
Known for: Orchestral music
Recommended listening: *Scheherazade*

Rossini, Gioacchino (1792-1868)

Country: Italy
Known for: Opera
Recommended listening: *The Barber of Seville*

Saint-Saëns, Camille (1835-1921)

Country: France
Known for: Orchestral music
Recommended listening: *Symphony No. 3 in C Minor, Op. 78, "Organ"*

Sarasate, Pablo (1844-1908)

Country: Spain
Known for: Violin music
Recommended listening: *Zigeunerweisen, Op. 20*

Schubert, Franz (1797-1828)

- His admirers would hold social gatherings in their homes at which the music of Schubert would be performed. These events were called "Schubertiaden" (Schubertiades). The guests would often give Schubert money as a result of these events. He was a very bad money manager, so the generosity of others helped him stay financially afloat.[9]

---

9 Peter Clive, *Schubert and His World: A Biographical Dictionary* (New York: Oxford University Press, 1997), xx–xxiv.

A Schubertiade with Schubert at the piano; a painting by Julius Schmid (1897).

<u>Country:</u> Austria
<u>Known for:</u> Lieder
<u>Recommended listening:</u> "Der Doppelgänger" from *Schwanengesang, D. 957*

Schumann, Clara (1819-1896)

- Her father wanted her to have a career as a concert pianist—a very unusual parental wish for this time period.[10]
- She was renowned as a concert pianist. She toured Europe frequently as a performer.
- As a piano teacher, she had many accomplished pupils.
- She was the mother of eight.

<u>Country:</u> Germany
<u>Known for:</u> Piano music
<u>Recommended listening:</u> *Piano Concerto in A minor, Op. 7*

---

10 Michael Musgrave, *The Life of Schumann* (New York: Cambridge, 2011), 75.

Schumann, Robert (1810-1856)

- He had planned on a career as a concert pianist, but, after injuring his pinky fingers irreparably, he turned his efforts toward composition. (He was injured after he invented a spring device to strengthen his pinky fingers in an effort to play with as much power as Franz Liszt, a pianist he admired greatly.) [11]
- Fell in love with his piano teacher's daughter when she was seventeen. Her father was opposed to the marriage but said they could marry if they waited until she was twenty-one. They eloped the night before her twenty-first birthday.
- Had a mental illness (likely bipolar disorder) and committed himself to an asylum for the last two years of his life.

Country: Germany
Known for: Character pieces
Recommended listening: *Carnaval, Op. 9*

Sibelius, Jean (1865-1957)

Country: Finland
Known for: Symphony
Recommended listening: *Symphony No. 2 in D Major, Op. 43*

Smetana, Bedřich (1824-1884)

Country: Czech Republic
Known for: Orchestral program music
Recommended listening: "Vltava" from *Má vlast (My Country)*

Strauss I, Johann (1804-1849)

Country: Austria
Known for: Marches
Recommended listening: *Radetzky March, Op. 228*

---

11 Dietrich Fischer-Dieskau, *Robert Schumann Words and Music: The Vocal Compositions* (Portland: Amadeus Press, 1988), 30.

Strauss II, Johann (1825-1899)

Country: Austria
Known for: Waltzes
Recommended listening: *Pizzicato-Polka*

Strauss, Richard (1864-1949)

Country: Germany
Known for: Tone Poem
Recommended listening: *Till Eulenspiegel's lustige Streiche*

Tchaikovsky, Pyotr Ilyich (1840-1893)

- A wealthy railroad heiress, Nadezhda von Meck, admired Tchaikovsky's compositions and began to provide him a yearly allowance so he wouldn't have to worry about money and could, therefore, concentrate on composing. They had a thirteen-year letter-writing relationship but never spoke face to face. They felt it would ruin their relationship if they ever met. Then, when she had some financial trouble, she quit writing to him.[12]
- Died of drinking unboiled water during a cholera epidemic. Scholars debate whether he did this to commit suicide or was forced to hasten his own death to prevent a scandal (involving a previous homosexual relationship with a member of the nobility).[13]

Country: Russia
Known for: Ballet
Recommended listening: *Nutcracker*

Verdi, Giuseppe (1813-1901)

- After writing operas for many years, he retired in 1870 and enjoyed his wealth and his successful farm. About fifteen years after his retirement, he wrote two more operas, one comic (*Falstaff*) and one serious (*Otello*). He lived another fifteen years after that.[14]

---

12 Michael Steen, *The Lives and Times of the Great Composers* (New York: Oxford, 2005), 681–682.
13 Roland John Wiley, *Tchaikovsky* (New York: Oxford, 2009) 440–444.
14 Stanley Sadie, ed., *Verdi and His Operas* (London: MacMillan, 2000), 205–206, 214–215.

Casa di Riposo per Musicisti in Milan, Italy; known as Casa Verdi by its residents.

- When he died, he left money to numerous charities. Perhaps the most impressive charitable act began before he died. He oversaw the building of a large home in Milan that had a chapel, a concert hall, a dining room, a ballet studio, rehearsal halls, and lots of apartments. It was built as a retirement home for musicians, conductors, and dancers who had nowhere else to go. He also left behind a sizable endowed fund to keep the home running for many years. After his death, he was buried in a tomb in the courtyard. The home is still in operation to this day.[15]

<u>Country:</u> Italy
<u>Known for:</u> Opera
<u>Recommended listening:</u> *Aida*

Wagner, Richard (1813–1883)

- His most famous work, *Der Ring des Nibelungen*, called "The Ring Cycle" for those in the know, is a cycle of four operas based on the same legends and mythology as those that inspired J. R. R. Tolkien when he wrote his book series *The Lord of*

---

15 Scott L. Balthazar, ed. *The Cambridge Companion to Verdi* (New York: Cambridge, 2004) 13–14.

the Rings. Although they share the same basic source, The Ring Cycle is not a musical version of *The Lord of the Rings*. The four music dramas (operas) that make up The Ring Cycle are 1) *Das Rheingold*, 2) *Die Walküre*, 3) *Siegfried*, and 4) *Götterdämmerung*.

Austrian soprano Anna Bahr- Mildenburg as Brünnhilde in Richard Wagner's *Die Walküre*. Copyright in the Public Domain.

- The cliché of a woman wearing a Viking helmet and holding a sword and shield as a symbol of "opera" comes from the Ring Cycle.[16]
- Wagner was so admired by King Ludwig II of Bavaria that he was given the necessary funds to build his dream opera house in Bayreuth, Germany.[17] The Ring Cycle is performed almost every summer in Bayreuth; over 500,000 people try to obtain tickets, but only 58,000 are available each year. Obtaining tickets is an arduous process involving yearly applications (if you miss applying one year, your name moves to the bottom of the waiting list). The wait to purchase tickets has been known to take up to ten years.

<u>Country:</u> Germany
<u>Known for:</u> Music drama
<u>Recommended listening:</u> *Tannhäuser*, particularly the overture.

Weber, Carl Maria von (1786-1826)

<u>Country:</u> Germany
<u>Known for:</u> Opera
<u>Recommended listening:</u> *Der Freischütz*

Widor, Charles-Marie (1844-1937)

<u>Country:</u> France

---

16   Sam Abel, *Opera in the Flesh* (Boulder: Westview, 1996), 12.
17   Peter Burbidge and Richard Sutton, eds. *The Wagner Companion* (Boston: Faber, 1979), 426.

Known for: Organ music
Recommended listening: *Organ Symphony No. 5 in F Minor, Op. 42, No. 1*

Wolf, Hugo (1860-1903)

Country: Austria
Known for: Lieder
Recommended listening: *Eichendorff-Lieder*, especially "Verschwiegene Liebe"

Ysaÿe, Eugène (1858-1931)

Country: Belgium
Known for: Violin music
Recommended listening: *Violin Sonata in A Minor, Op. 27, No. 2*

SECTION 7

TWENTIETH CENTURY (1900-2000)

The Twentieth Century is a time of great change in the world of art music. There is more variety in genres, forms, and techniques than ever before. In fact, there are so many diverse types of music, the century should probably be divided into smaller "eras." A major influence in the Twentieth Century is the fact that every composer was pushing boundaries in an effort to do something completely "new."

Instruments in the Twentieth Century

Woodwind, brass, string, and keyboard instruments continue to be used and perfected during the Twentieth Century. In addition, there is a huge increase in variety with the advent of electronic instruments and various modifications to standard instruments.

Performance Venues in the Twentieth Century

The opera house, concert hall, and recital hall are the main performance venues in the Twentieth Century. The church continues to be a venue for sacred music. With the changes in the importance of nobility throughout Europe during the Romantic Era, the concept of court composers dies out in the Twentieth Century. Chamber music, with few exceptions, moves completely out of the chamber and into the concert hall and recital hall.

CHAPTER

NINETEEN

Styles and Compositional and Performance Techniques in the Twentieth Century

Style: Impressionism

Impressionism is a term borrowed from the art world. In Impressionist art, painters are not trying to achieve a completely realistic depiction but merely their impression of the subject—they're trying to capture a moment in time. Often the focus is more on how light and shadow affect the way one perceives an object rather than on the object itself. In general, Impressionist painters don't blend their colors on their palette; instead they use swipes or dots of color on the canvas that, when viewed from a certain distance, blend together—in the viewer's eye—to create the color desired by the painter. Impressionist art seems to shimmer; there are no hard edges to any particular object.

Impressionism in music is when the composer attempts to convey an impression of something, like the visual artists, trying to capture a specific moment in time. This is not program music, *per se*, because it does not attempt to tell a story. It exists in the grey area between absolute music and program music—leaning heavily toward program

Impressionist painting: *Le Portail et la tour Saint-Romain, plein soleil* (Rouen Cathedral) by Claude Monet.

music. There is a dream-like quality to Impressionist music. This quality is achieved through varied techniques unique to this style of music:

- Note clusters: Impressionist music features clusters of notes—oftentimes dissonant clusters—that blend into a new "color," just as Impressionist art features clusters of actual colors. In the context of music, these clusters are rarely perceived as overly dissonant.

- Unusual scales: Composers often used nontraditional scales to achieve the dream-like quality desired—particularly the **whole-tone scale** (all whole steps, no half steps) and the **pentatonic scale** (a scale that only has five pitches before reaching the octave).

- Static harmony: Instead of the dominant-tonic tension so frequent in previous time periods, Impressionist music employs chords that do not follow those tendencies. Just as whole-tone scales are used instead of major or minor scales, chords used in non-traditional ways add to the static quality of Impressionist music.

Genres that feature Impressionism:

Any genre can feature Impressionism. Maurice Ravel and Claude Debussy specialized in orchestral music and solo piano pieces (character pieces).

Is Impressionist style used in music composed after the Twentieth Century?

No. In fact, many textbooks give Impressionism its OWN time period, overlapping with the end of the Romantic Era and the beginning of the Twentieth Century. This style was used mostly by the composers Debussy and Ravel.

FURTHER INVESTIGATION:

1. Do an online image search for paintings by Monet, Renoir, Degas, Pissarro, or Seurat to see some different styles of Impressionist art. Notice the way different artists choose different subjects (for instance, Monet prefers architecture and nature, while Degas prefers ballet dancers). Notice how the colors blend in your eye as opposed to on the canvas. Then listen to some Impressionist music to see how the two mediums are similar.

2. Listen to recordings by the two best-known Impressionist composers—Debussy and Ravel—to see how they are similar or different.

SUGGESTED LISTENING:

- Claude Debussy's *Prelude to the Afternoon of a Faun*
- Debussy's *La mer*

- Maurice Ravel's *Jeux d'eau*
- Ravel's *Valses nobles et sentimentales*

Style: Expressionism

In the art world, Expressionism refers to nontraditional painting techniques and the use of extreme colors to express and explore the artist's own psychological makeup—often in disturbing ways. **Expressionism** in art music is non-tonal or nontraditional music that deals with harsh emotions or disturbing subject matter and uses nontraditional musical techniques to convey this.

Genres that feature Expressionism:
Any genre can feature Expressionism.

Is Expressionist style used in music composed after the Twentieth Century?
Yes, but it is no longer referred to as Expressionism. Composers continue to use nontraditional and non-tonal techniques, but the art style upon which it is based no longer exists.

Expressionist painting: *Mutter und Kind* by Egon Schiele.
Copyright in the Public Domain.

FURTHER INVESTIGATION:

1. Do an online image search for paintings by Munch, Kandinsky, Schiele, Kokoschka, Klee, or even Schönberg (the composer—who also painted!) to see some different styles of Expressionistic art. Notice the subject matter, color choices, and painting techniques. Then listen to some Expressionist music to see how the two mediums are similar.
2. Listen to recordings of Schönberg, Berg, and Webern to hear different approaches to Expressionistic music.

SUGGESTED LISTENING:

- Alban Berg's *Wozzeck*
- Arnold Schönberg's *Pierrot Lunaire*
- Anton Webern's *Four Pieces for Orchestra, Op. 10*

Style: Nationalism

As in the Romantic Era, Nationalism is a musical style in which the composer's nationality or homeland is reflected in some way within his/her art music. (See entry on Nationalism in the Romantic Era for more specific information.) Remember that national anthems and patriotic songs (in most cases) are not considered to be art music.

Genres that feature Nationalism:
Any genre is possible.

Does the style of Nationalism exist after the Twentieth Century?
Yes. Many composers continue to incorporate nationalistic concepts into their compositions.

FURTHER INVESTIGATION:

1. Listen to recordings of nationalistic art music from one of the countries you have lived in or traveled to. Does the music remind you of that country?
2. Compare a piece of nationalistic art music from one country to a nationalistic piece of art music from another country. How are they different or similar?
3. Compose your own art music arrangement of a folk or dance tune from your homeland.

SUGGESTED LISTENING:

- Mexico:
  - Carlos Chávez's *Caballos de Vapor*
- Spain:
  - Joaquín Rodrigo's *Concierto Andaluz*
- Sweden:
  - Hugo Alfvén's *Midsommarvaka*
- United Kingdom:
  - Ralph Vaughan Williams' *Five Variants on Dives and Lazarus*, *In the Fen Country*, and *Symphony No. 9*
- United States:
  - Aaron Copland's *Appalachian Spring*, *Billy the Kid*, and *Rodeo*

- Charles Ives' *They Are There, A Symphony: New England Holidays*, and *Variations on "America"*
- George Gershwin's *Rhapsody in Blue, Porgy and Bess*, and *Three Preludes*

Compositional Technique: Atonality/Bitonality/Polytonality

Tonality is when a particular piece of music has a tonal center (tonic), or, in other words, when a piece is composed using a certain key (or scale).

Atonality: In the Twentieth Century, many composers, seeking to do something innovative, compose music with a complete (or mostly) lack of a tonal center—no tonic.

Bitonality: Bitonality is when a composer uses two tonal centers (or keys) at the same time—for instance, the melody might be in A major and the harmony might be in B-flat major. Individually they are perceived as consonant and tonal, but together they are dissonant and bitonal.

Polytonality: Polytonality is when there are two or more tonal centers (or keys) present at the same time. Bitonality is a type of polytonality.

Is atonality/bitonality/polytonality used in music composed after the Twentieth Century?

Yes.

FURTHER INVESTIGATION:

1. Look at the score for *Mikrokosmos* by Béla Bartók and notice how on certain pieces, the right hand is written in one key and the left hand in a completely different key.
2. Look at the score for the third movement of *Piano Sonata No.2 "Concord, Mass., 1840–60"* by Charles Ives. At the beginning (after one measure) is a section of bitonality.

SUGGESTED LISTENING:

- Béla Bartók's *14 Bagatelles, Op. 6, BB 50*
- Darius Milhaud's "Corcovado" from *Saudades do Brazil*
- Igor Stravinsky's *Rite of Spring*

Compositional Technique: Polyrhythm/Polymeter/ Irregular Meter/Mixed Meter

Polyrhythm refers to two contrasting rhythms occurring at the same time, for instance triplets against duples, like this:

Or polyrhythm can be more complex, like groupings of four against groupings of six, or five against seven or eight, like so:

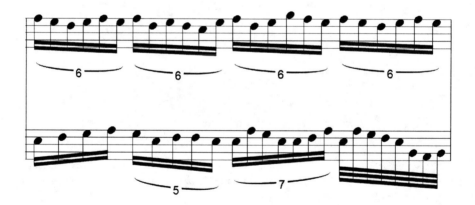

Polymeter, on the other hand, is when multiple meters are occurring at the same time in different lines. In this next example, the top line is in 4/4 meter, the second line is in 3/4 meter and the bottom line is in 3/8 meter; even though they're different meters, they fill the same amount of time.

Irregular meters are meters that are not divisible by two or three. For instance, this is an example of 11/16 meter (eleven sixteenth notes per measure):

Other irregular meter possibilities are 5/8, 7/8, and 13/16.

Mixed meter refers to a piece of music in which the meter changes frequently. This keeps the conductor of an orchestra quite busy, not to mention the performers themselves. Here is an example of mixed meter:

This example begins with a measure of four eighth notes, then a measure of two eighth notes, then five eighth notes, and finally three quarter notes. Note that this example also features irregular meters.

Are these techniques used in music composed after the Twentieth Century?
   Yes.

FURTHER INVESTIGATION:

1. Obtain a score for any of Igor Stravinsky's ballets. Pick five or six pages at random; you will almost certainly find examples of polyrhythm, irregular meters, or mixed meters.
2. Obtain a score for Paul Hindemith's *Clarinet Sonata*. Notice the use of polymeter.

SUGGESTED LISTENING:

• Igor Stravinsky's *L'histoire du Soldat*
• Stravinsky's *Petrouchka*
• Paul Hindemith's *Kammermusik No. 1, Op. 24*
• Béla Bartók's *Bluebeard's Castle*

Performance Technique: *Sprechstimme*

Sprechstimme is a technique in which a singer does not sing the pitches indicated but instead speaks the pitches. This is indicated in the music by putting a little "x" through the stem of the notes to be spoken on pitch, like this:

when   I   feel____   the   si - lence

In general, as long as singers get close to the pitch indicated, that is good enough. If you listen to multiple recordings of a piece that features *sprechstimme*, each one will sound different because each singer hits the pitches with varying degrees of success.

Is sprechstimme used in music composed after the Twentieth Century?
Yes.

FURTHER INVESTIGATION:

Obtain a score of a piece that uses *sprechstimme*. Note the way it is indicated: either on the note stems or some other way. Listen to multiple recordings of the same piece to hear each singer's interpretation.

SUGGESTED LISTENING:

- Arnold Schönberg's *Moses und Aron, A Survivor from Warsaw*, and *Pierrot lunaire*
- Alban Berg's *Lulu*

Compositional Technique: Serialism/Twelve-Tone System

Serialism is a compositional technique in which a specific "series" of notes is used in order to avoid a sense of tonality. It came about largely as a result of Arnold Schönberg's efforts to write atonal music more easily. After composing atonal music for a time, he became frustrated with how much effort it took to avoid a tonic. He came up with a system to ensure that no particular note would be repeated too frequently (i.e., sound like a tonic). He called it the **Twelve-Tone System**. Here's how it works:

- First, create a twelve-tone row. On the piano keyboard, the number of black and white keys between any note and its octave is twelve (A, A#, B, C, C#, D, D#, E, F, F#, G, G#). To create a row, composers draw the twelve tones out of a figurative hat in random order. Here is what a twelve-tone row could look like:

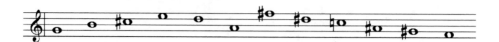

- Once the twelve-tone row has been created, you can begin composing. The rule is that you must use the notes in the row in order. Therefore, you *could* choose to use the first three notes as a chord and the next three notes as the melody, then the next three notes as the next chord and the final three notes as the melody, like so:

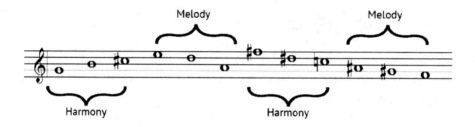

How this grouping would look on the printed music:

In this example, every note is still in the treble clef, but you can change octaves, clefs, and rhythms at will. The only restriction is that you have to use the notes in row order. Then you start over again at the beginning of the row, grouping the notes differently but *always* in order.

Schönberg knew that one single row would yield only a finite number of options, so he decided that you could turn the row upside down (inversion), backwards (retrograde), and upside down and backwards (retrograde inversion). Now there are four rows available for use all based on the original, randomly-generated row. When you invert a row, the row keeps its shape by maintaining the intervals between each note. Here is an original row followed by an inverted row.

ORIGINAL ROW

INVERSION

When you invert a row, you have the freedom to choose the note on which to start the row—as long as the intervals between notes are maintained, it still has the correct shape. This means that there are twelve possible inversions of the original row. Schönberg decided that the original could also be started on any of the twelve pitches, so there were twelve versions of the original row as well, and the retrograde row and the retrograde inversion row. He came up with a mathematical matrix to be able to quickly figure out his rows:

PRIME ROW →

0	4	6	9	7	2	11	8	5	3	1	10
8	0	2	5	3	10	7	4	1	11	9	6
6	10	0	3	1	8	5	2	11	9	7	4
3	7	9	0	10	5	2	11	8	6	4	1
5	9	11	2	0	7	4	1	10	8	6	3
10	2	4	7	5	0	9	6	3	1	11	8
1	5	7	10	8	3	0	9	6	4	2	11
4	8	10	1	11	6	3	0	9	7	5	2
7	11	1	4	2	9	6	3	0	10	8	5
9	1	3	6	4	11	8	5	2	0	10	7
11	3	5	8	6	1	10	7	4	2	0	9
2	6	8	11	9	4	1	10	7	5	3	0

INVERTED ROW ↓ (left side)

RETROGRADE INVERTED ROW ↑ (right side)

RETROGRADE ROW ← (bottom)

With a **twelve-tone matrix,** there are forty-eight possible rows to use in the creation of a piece of serialist music. If composing a work for orchestra, one of the inverted rows could be used in the violin melody, a retrograde inverted row could be used in the woodwinds, a prime row could be used for the brass, and a retrograde row could be used for the low strings. The possibilities are endless. The creativity of the composer comes into play as he/she decides which rows to use at what time.

Is serialism used in music composed after the Twentieth Century?

Yes. And not only that, but admirers of Schönberg took serialism much further by applying serialist rows to other musical elements—rows of dynamics, rows of note durations, rows of tempo markings, etc.

FURTHER INVESTIGATION:

1. Create your own twelve-tone row and compose a short piece using only that row over and over.
2. Create retrograde, inverted, and retrograde inverted rows from your original row and compose a short piece using all four rows.
3. Search online for "twelve-tone matrix generator," create your own matrix, and compose a short piece using at least five of the rows from your matrix.

SUGGESTED LISTENING:

- Alban Berg's *Violin Concerto*
- Arnold Schönberg's *Wind Quintet, Op. 26*
- Anton Webern's *Cantata No. 1, Op. 29*
- Igor Stravinsky's *Agon* (Some parts of this work are not twelve-tone.)

Compositional Technique: Indeterminacy/Aleatory Music/ Chance Music

Indeterminacy is a technique used in compositions in which part of the performance is not pre-determined by the composer—certain elements are left up to the whims of the performers. This kind of music is also called **aleatory music** (from the Latin word for "gambling") and **chance music.**

Some examples of indeterminacy:

- A piece in which there is a measure with a number of notes with instructions for the player to play those notes in whatever order or speed they choose to until the conductor indicates it is time to move on
- A piece in which the performers are instructed to make up their own dynamics throughout the entire piece
- A piece in which the composer provides a strange drawing with random lines, squiggles, and shapes and gives no instructions to the performer(s) except that it is indeed music and must be performed

Is indeterminacy used in music composed after the Twentieth Century?

Yes. In fact, the most popular American composer of choral music in the twenty-first century, Eric Whitacre, uses indeterminate sections in his compositions (not a lot, but here and there).

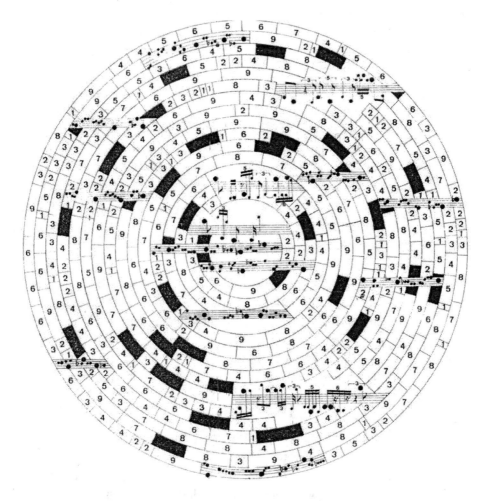

An indeterminate score by León Calancha.

FURTHER INVESTIGATION:

1. Obtain scores of music featuring indeterminacy and note the endless possibilities in those sections.
2. Read John Cage's instructions to the performers in his compositions *Imaginary Landscape No. 4* and *Concert for Piano and Orchestra*.
3. Go to johncage.org and follow the link "Database of Works" to read descriptions of them. Many of his compositions contain chance elements. Some of them are entirely indeterminate.

SUGGESTED LISTENING:

Technically, any indeterminate piece that has been recorded is no longer indeterminate, because there is no longer the element of chance. Despite this fact, there are plenty of recordings of John Cage's works, including his most famous (infamous) indeterminate composition: *4'33"*

Compositional Technique: Prepared Piano

John Cage developed **prepared piano** by experimenting with inserting various objects between the strings of a piano to see how it would affect the sound. He composed many pieces with lengthy instructions itemizing 1) exactly which objects—nails, plastic washers, screws, nuts, bolts—should be inserted into the piano; 2) which strings should be altered in this manner; and 3) precise measurements as to the point on the string at which the object should be placed. After preparing the piano, the performer plays the piece using the normal piano keyboard, but the sounds that emanate from the piano sound anything but normal, often replicating the sound of bells, gongs, metallic thunks, and Eastern percussion instruments. The effects of a prepared piano are as varied as the objects that can be used.

Is the technique of prepared piano used in music composed after the Twentieth Century?
Yes, and it has found its way into pop music as well as art music.

FURTHER INVESTIGATION:

1. At johncage.org, there is a link for "Prepared Piano App." It is free for some devices. Download it and create a prepared piano piece of your own!
2. Do an online search for "prepared piano." Watch videos and listen to recordings.
3. Find scores of prepared piano pieces and look at the instruction lists.

SUGGESTED LISTENING:

- John Cage's *A Book of Music (for two prepared pianos)*
- Cage's *Daughters of the Lonesome Isle*
- Ruedi Hausermann's *Schwank*

Performance Technique: Extended Technique

Extended technique is a term used to describe anything an instrumentalist does to create sound that is outside the normal sounds of their instrument. Here are some examples and how they are notated in music:

Multiphonics: This is when an instrument that was intended to create only one pitch at a time, through a variety of means, is able to create more than one pitch at a time. This includes all brass and woodwind instruments, as well as the human voice. This does not include strings or keyboard instruments because they are made to create more than one pitch at a time.

Instruments as percussion: Any non-percussion instrument (including vocals) can be struck in many different ways to create different sounds. This can include striking the body of a string instrument; slapping a cupped hand against the opening of a brass instrument mouthpiece, which creates a popping noise; and clicking the keys or valves of wind instruments. Note: *Pizzicato* is not an extended technique.

Prepared instruments: Similar to prepared piano—inserting objects into the instruments so they react differently than normal. Examples of this include inserting objects into the strings of the violin, viola, cello, bass, guitar, or harp; and various unusual mutes for woodwind and brass instruments.

Flutter-tongue: This technique consists of fluttering the tongue, like rolling an "r" sound, while blowing on a wind instrument. Other methods to achieve a similar effect are 1) to make the gargling noise in the back of the throat while blowing, or 2) humming or singing while blowing.

Pitch-bends and smears: A pitch bend is when an instrumentalist plays a pitch and then, through various techniques, is able to "bend" the pitch downward. A smear is when a performer moves from one pitch to another in one continuous smear—the normal step-wise progression is not heard.

FURTHER INVESTIGATION:

Search online for "extended techniques" and the name of an instrument. If there are video results, watch a few. If there are only text results, read a few to get an idea of what goes into performing extended techniques.

SUGGESTED LISTENING:

- William Bolcom's *The Serpent's Kiss*
- John Eaton's *Some Specters*
- Greg Pattillo's *Three Beats for Beatbox Flute*

Compositional Technique: Quoting/Borrowing

Quoting and **borrowing** are very similar in that they both use preexisting music in a new composition. Literally, quoting is when a composer uses a preexisting piece or fragment of a piece *note for note*—exactly as it was composed—within his/her own composition. Borrowing, on the other hand, is when a composer uses a preexisting piece or fragment of a piece within his/her own composition but arranges it or varies it in some way. It is still recognized as the initial piece/fragment, but the composer has reinvented it.

FURTHER INVESTIGATION:

Search online for "borrowing in classical music" and read some of the articles that you find.

SUGGESTED LISTENING:

- Luciano Berio's *Sinfonia*, (third movement) quotes the third movement of Mahler's *Symphony No. 2, "Resurrection."*
- Sergei Rachmaninoff's *Fate* borrows the first few notes of Beethoven's *Symphony No. 5.*
- Charles Ives' *Symphony No. 2* quotes/borrows numerous hymns, patriotic songs, folk songs, and art music.

Compositional Technique: Electro-Acoustic Music

Twentieth-Century composers use electric devices to enhance or create music. When electronic means are employed to create music, the term **electro-acoustic** is used. Live performance may or may not be part of an electro-acoustic music performance. When attending an electro-acoustic concert, it may strike the audience as initially odd that some of the pieces that are entirely electronically-generated are performed with an empty stage. The audience sits, listens to the electro-acoustic music emanating from a sound system and at the end they applaud the empty stage. Audiences usually cope better with electro-acoustic concerts that have live performers in addition to the electro-acoustic music. There are many types of electro-acoustic music:

Electronically generated music:
- Tape Music: In the mid-Twentieth Century, electronically generated sounds were captured on magnetic tape.
- Synthesizers: A musical instrument, usually attached to a piano-like keyboard, that creates electronically generated sounds. Synthesizers can imitate various sounds and other instruments.
- Computer Music: Tape music was replaced by "computer music" when computers began to be used to create electronically generated sounds.
- Sampling: Synthesizers and computers can both "sample," or record, other sounds and reproduce them at any pitch.

Musique concrète:
Recorded sounds that are played back as part of a musical performance are referred to as musique concrète. These sounds can be manipulated, fragmented, sped up, slowed down, or played back exactly as they would normally sound.

FURTHER INVESTIGATION:

Search online for the following electronic instruments: theremin, ondes martenot, and kraakdoos. Read about or watch videos demonstrating each of them.

SUGGESTED LISTENING:

- Paul Dresher's *Concerto for Violin and Electro-Acoustic Band*
- Paul Lansky's *The Lesson*
- Charles Wuorinen's *Time's Encomium*

CHAPTER

TWENTY
Genres of the Twentieth Century

Chamber Music

Chamber music continues to be a living genre in the Twentieth Century. The freedom from form and structure that occurred in the Romantic Era continues to affect chamber music in this time period. Also, new instruments and new combinations of traditional instruments become accepted in this time period. As mentioned earlier, chamber music had officially moved out of the private chamber and into recital halls and concert halls.

Performing forces for chamber music:
All the chamber genres mentioned from the Baroque up to this point are still valid performing forces. Two notable "new" chamber genres—the brass quintet and the Pierrot ensemble—have their own entries below.

FURTHER INVESTIGATION:

1. Enter random instruments and the words "Twentieth Century chamber music" into an online search to see the variety of combinations. Listen to them.
2. Watch or listen to some Twentieth Century chamber music and some chamber music from an earlier time period. Note the stylistic differences.

SUGGESTED LISTENING:

*   Dmitri Shostakovich's *Piano Trio No. 2 in E minor, Op. 67*
*   Béla Bartók's *Contrasts (for violin, clarinet, and piano)*

- Darius Milhaud's *String Quartet No. 7, Op. 87*
- Karlheinz Stockhausen's *Helikopter-Streichquartett*

Brass Quintet

A quintet made up of two trumpets, one horn, one trombone, and one tuba. Repertoire for **brass quintets** is mostly arrangements and transcriptions of pieces composed for other ensembles, but many composers compose original pieces for this chamber ensemble as well.

FURTHER INVESTIGATION:

Watch or listen to a brass quintet piece composed in the Twentieth Century.

SUGGESTED LISTENING:

- Frigyes Hidas' *Training Patterns for Brass Quintet*
- Malcolm Arnold's *Brass Quintet No. 1, Op. 73*
- André Previn's *4 Outings for Brass*

Pierrot Ensemble

A **Pierrot ensemble** is a chamber music group made up of one flute, one clarinet, one violin, one cello, and one piano. Sometimes a vocalist or a percussionist is added to the group. This chamber ensemble received its name because the core group plus vocalist were used by Arnold Schönberg in his famous chamber song cycle *Pierrot lunaire*. Because of the influential nature of Schönberg's work, many professional chamber ensembles who specialize in twentieth-century music use this same ensemble. The Pierrot Ensemble is a standard group at most universities with an emphasis on contemporary art music.

FURTHER INVESTIGATION:

Search online for "Pierrot Ensemble." Watch videos of performances featuring Pierrot Ensembles.

SUGGESTED LISTENING:

- Arnold Schönberg's *Pierrot lunaire*
- Morton Feldman's *The Viola in My Life (Pierrot Ensemble plus percussion and viola soloist)*
- Peter Maxwell-Davies *Eight Songs for a Mad King* (Pierrot Ensemble plus percussion and baritone voice)

Symphony

The genre of the symphony continues to be popular in the Twentieth Century but, of course, is less structured than before. The size of the orchestra can vary widely depending on the composer.

FURTHER INVESTIGATION:

1. Watch or listen to a symphony composed in the Twentieth Century.
2. Watch or listen to at least a half hour (each) of a Twentieth Century symphony and a symphony from an earlier time period. Note the stylistic differences.

SUGGESTED LISTENING:

- Heitor Villa-Lobos' *Symphony No. 6, "On the Outline of the Mountains of Brazil"*
- Sergei Prokofiev's *Symphony No. 7 in C sharp minor, Op. 131*
- Alan Hovhaness' *Symphony No. 31, Op. 294*

Opera

The definition of opera in the Twentieth Century is the same as in previous time periods, but again, the Twentieth Century is a time for rule-breaking. Anything is possible.

FURTHER INVESTIGATION:

1. Watch an entire Twentieth Century opera. Many online sources have complete operas available for viewing, but make certain that you pick an option that has subtitles so you know what is going on. Alternatively, if subtitles are not provided, you can acquire a libretto (with the original text and an English translation) to follow along with.

2. Watch at least a half hour (each) of an opera from the Twentieth Century and an opera from an earlier time period to see how they differ in style, structure, and form.

SUGGESTED LISTENING:

- Virgil Thomson's *Four Saints in Three Acts*
- Benjamin Britten's *Peter Grimes*
- Sergei Prokofiev's *The Love for Three Oranges*

Ballet

Ballet continues to be a vital genre throughout the Twentieth Century.

FURTHER INVESTIGATION:

1. Watch or listen to a ballet composed in the Twentieth Century.
2. Watch or listen to at least a half hour (each) of a Twentieth Century ballet and a ballet from an earlier time period. Note the stylistic differences.

SUGGESTED LISTENING:

- Darius Milhaud's *Le bœuf sur le toit, Op.58*
- Aram Khachaturian's *Gayane*
- Igor Stravinsky's *Pulcinella*

Concerto

The genre of Concerto continues to be popular in the Twentieth Century.

FURTHER INVESTIGATION:

1. Watch or listen to a concerto composed in the Twentieth Century.
2. Watch or listen to a Twentieth Century concerto and a concerto from an earlier time period. Note the stylistic differences.

SUGGESTED LISTENING:

- Henri Tomasi's *Trumpet Concerto*
- Pierre Max Dubois' *Alto Saxophone Concerto*
- Alban Berg's *Violin Concerto*

Mass

Masses are still composed for the church, but also for the concert hall.

FURTHER INVESTIGATION:

1. Watch or listen to a Mass composed in the Twentieth Century.
2. Watch or listen to at least a half hour (each) of a Twentieth Century Mass and a Mass from an earlier time period. Note the stylistic differences.

SUGGESTED LISTENING:

- Frederick Delius' *A Mass of Life*
- Francis Poulenc's *Mass in G Major*
- Ariel Ramirez's *Misa Criolla*

CHAPTER TWENTY-ONE

Composers of the Twentieth Century

Arnold, Malcolm (1921-2006)

Country: England
Known for: Neo-romantic music
Recommended listening: *Clarinet Sonatina in G Minor, Op. 29*

Auric, Georges (1899-1983)

Country: France
Known for: Ballet
Recommended listening: *Les facheux*

Babbitt, Milton (1916-2011)

Country: USA
Known for: Serialism
Recommended listening: *String Quartet No. 5*

Barber, Samuel (1910-1981)

Country: USA
Known for: Neo-romantic music
Recommended listening: *Second Essay for Orchestra, Op. 17*

Bartók, Béla (1881-1945)

<u>Country:</u> Hungary
<u>Known for:</u> Folk-influenced
<u>Recommended listening:</u> *Román ni táncok (Romanian Folk Dances), BB 76: No. 1*

Beach, Amy (1867-1944)

<u>Country:</u> USA
<u>Known for:</u> Piano music
<u>Recommended listening:</u> *Dreaming*

Berg, Alban (1885-1935)

• He was a student of Arnold Schönberg and utilized similar compositional techniques to his teacher's, including *sprechstimme* and atonality, but leaned much more toward a Romantic orchestra and sound than Schönberg's.[1]
• A lifelong hypochondriac, he died of an infected bug bite.[2]

<u>Country:</u> Austria
<u>Known for:</u> Opera
<u>Recommended listening:</u> *Lulu*, especially "Wer ist das" from Act III, scene 2.

Berio, Luciano (1925-2003)

<u>Country:</u> Italy
<u>Known for:</u> Avant-garde
<u>Recommended listening:</u> *Sinfonia*

Bernstein, Leonard (1918-1990)

• He became famous as a conductor when he stepped in at the last minute for the ill conductor of the New York Philharmonic for a live radio broadcast.[3]

---

1 Anthony Pople, ed. *The Cambridge Companion to Berg* (New York: Cambridge, 1997), 150, 249.
2 Christopher Hailey, ed. *Alban Berg and His World* (Princeton: Princeton, 2010), 26.
3 Burton Bernstein and Barbara B. Haws, *Leonard Bernstein: American Original* (New York: Collins, 2008), 4.

- He was appointed conductor or guest conductor with some of the top orchestras in the world, including the Israel Philharmonic, London Symphony Orchestra, and the Vienna Philharmonic.[4]
- He often incorporated jazz and pop elements into art music compositions.[5]

Leonard Bernstein
Copyright in the Public Domain.

Country: USA
Aside from *West Side Story*—a musical theatre piece—Bernstein is known for: Choral music
Recommended listening: *Mass*

Birtwistle, Harrison (b. 1934)

Country: England
Known for: Avant-garde
Recommended listening: *Endless Parade*

Boulez, Pierre (1925-2016)

Country: France
Known for: Aleatoric Music
Recommended listening: *Eclat*

Bozza, Eugène (1905-1991)

Country: France
Known for: Post-impressionism
Recommended listening: *Aria*

Britten, Benjamin (1913-1976)

Country: England
Known for: Opera
Recommended listening: *Peter Grimes*

---

4   Michael Freedland, *Leonard Bernstein* (London: Harrap, 1987), 98, 210, 229.
5   Jonathan Cott, *Dinner with Lenny: The Last Long Interview with Leonard Bernstein* (New York: Oxford, 2013), 15.

Cage, John (1912-1992)

John Cage
Copyright © Rob Bogaerts / Anefo (CC BY-SA 3.0) at https://commons.wikimedia.org/wiki/File:John_Cage_(1988).jpg.

- He loved to pose the question "What is music?" He was constantly challenging his listeners to recognize that any sound at all can be considered music. When asked if it bothered him when audience members made noise during a performance of a string quartet by Beethoven, he replied that he accepted audience noise as part of the music.[6]
- He was greatly impressed by his experience in an anechoic chamber (an echoless chamber). He could hear his heartbeat and a high-pitched hum. After leaving the chamber, he asked the technician what the high-pitched noise was and the technician said it was Cage's own central nervous system.[7]

Country: USA
Known for: Aleatory music
Recommended listening: *4'33"*

Canteloube, Joseph (1879-1957)

Country: France
Known for: Song cycle
Recommended listening: *Chants d'Auvergne*

Carter, Elliott (1908-2012)

Country: USA
Known for: Avant-garde
Recommended listening: *Mnemosyne*

Catán, Daniel (1949-2011)

Country: Mexico
Known for: Opera
Recommended listening: *Rappaccini's Daughter*

---

6   Richard Kostelanetz, *John Cage (ex)plain(ed)* (New York: Schirmer, 1996), 18.
7   David Revill, *The Roaring Silence* (New York: Arcade, 1992), 162–163.

Chávez, Carlos (1899-1978)

Country: Mexico
Known for: Nationalism
Recommended listening: *Sinfonía india*

Cooke, Arnold (1906-2005)

Country: England
Known for: Chamber music
Recommended listening: *Songs of Innocence*

Copland, Aaron (1900-1990)

- He studied with Nadia Boulanger (a great composition teacher) in Paris, who felt that the music he was writing as a student was not unique among the other European composers she worked with. She encouraged Copland to find his own voice in his music. As a result of her guidance, he became the best-known nationalistic American composer of all time.[8]

- After the many successes of his American works, he tried many other compositional styles including atonality and serialism.[9]

Aaron Copland at his piano.
Copyright in the Public Domain.

Country: USA
Known for: Ballet
Recommended listening: *Appalachian Spring*

---

8   James E. Wierzbicki, *Music in the Age of Anxiety: American Music in the Fifties* (Champaign: University of Illinois, 2016), 144.
9   Howard Pollack, *Aaron Copland: The Life and Work of an Uncommon Man* (New York: Henry Holt, 1999), 145–147.

Cowell, Henry (1897–1965)

<u>Country:</u> USA
<u>Known for:</u> Avant-garde
<u>Recommended listening:</u> *The Banshee*

Crumb, George (b. 1929)

• He likes to use instruments (and the human voice) in unusual ways. In one piece, *Ancient Voices of Children*, the vocalist has to sing through a long cardboard tube and has to sing directly into the piano, which causes the strings to resonate in sympathy. In another piece, instrumentalists are asked to hum, whistle, grunt, and play other instruments in addition to their own, including crystal glasses filled with different levels of water to create different pitches.[10]

<u>Country:</u> USA
<u>Known for:</u> Avant-garde chamber music
<u>Recommended listening:</u> *Black Angels (for electrified string quartet)*

Dallapiccola, Luigi (1904–1975)

<u>Country:</u> Italy
<u>Known for:</u> Serialism
<u>Recommended listening:</u> *Liriche Greche*

Davidovsky, Mario (b. 1934)

<u>Country:</u> Argentina
<u>Known for:</u> Electro-acoustic music
<u>Recommended listening:</u> *Synchronisms No. 6*

Davies, Peter Maxwell (1934–2016)

<u>Country:</u> England
<u>Known for:</u> Avant-garde
<u>Recommended listening:</u> *Eight Songs for a Mad King*

---

10 James McCalla, *Twentieth-Century Chamber Music* (New York: Schirmer, 1996), 98–100.

Debussy, Claude (1862-1918)

- He preferred to be compared to Symbolist poets rather than Impressionist painters, but the label Impressionist has stuck to him through the years.[11]

Country: France
Known for: Character pieces
Recommended listening: *La cathedrale engloutie*

Claude Debussy
Copyright in the Public Domain

Delius, Frederick (1862-1934)

Country: England
Known for: Impressionism
Recommended listening: *Sea Drift*

Dring, Madeleine (1923-1977)

Country: England
Known for: Chamber music
Recommended listening: *Trio for Flute, Oboe and Piano*

Durey, Louis (1888-1979)

Country: France
Known for: Character pieces
Recommended listening: *Two Pieces, Op. 7*

Duruflé, Maurice (1902-1986)

Country: France
Known for: Organ music
Recommended listening: *Suite, Op. 5*

---

11   Simon Trezise, ed. *The Cambridge Companion to Debussy* (Cambridge: Cambridge, 2003), 102, 124.

Dutilleux, Henri (1916-2013)

Country: France
Known for: Post-impressionism
Recommended listening: *Métaboles*

Enescu, George (1881-1955)

Country: Romania
Known for: Folk-influenced
Recommended listening: *Two Romanian Rhapsodies, Op. 11*

Falla, Manuel de (1876-1946)

Country: Spain
Known for: Impressionism
Recommended listening: *Noches en los jardines de Espana*

Farkas, Ferenc (1905-2000)

Country: Hungary
Known for: Folk-influenced
Recommended listening: *Gyumolcskosar (Fruit Basket)*

Feldman, Morton (1926-1987)

Country: USA
Known for: Aleatory
Recommended listening: *Patterns in a Chromatic Field*

Fine, Irving (1914-1962)

Country: USA
Known for: Neo-classical
Recommended listening: *Partita for Wind Quintet*

Finzi, Gerald (1901–1956)

<u>Country:</u> England
<u>Known for:</u> Song cycle
<u>Recommended listening:</u> *Let us Garlands Bring, Op. 18*

Floyd, Carlisle (b. 1926)

<u>Country:</u> USA
<u>Known for:</u> Opera
<u>Recommended listening:</u> *Susannah*

Françaix, Jean (1912–1997)

<u>Country:</u> France
<u>Known for:</u> Neo-classical
<u>Recommended listening:</u> *Wind Quintet No. 1*

Gaubert, Philippe (1879–1941)

<u>Country:</u> France
<u>Known for:</u> Flute music
<u>Recommended listening:</u> *Trois Aquarelles*

Gershwin, George (1898–1937)

- His first musical job was working as a performing salesman for a music publisher. Gershwin would sit at a piano, and customers would select sheet music (mostly Broadway show tunes) and bring them to him. He would sing and play the songs so they could decide if they wanted to purchase the music or not. It was while working here that he realized that he could probably write better show tunes than the ones he was demonstrating.[12]
- After writing musical theater for some time, he branched out into the art music realm and wrote art music works with a jazz influence including *An American in Paris* and the opera *Porgy and Bess*.

---

12   William G. Hyland, *George Gershwin: A New Biography* (Westport: Praeger, 2003), 17–19.

Country: USA
Aside from his musical theater (pop) works, he is known for: Orchestral music
Recommended listening: *Piano Concerto in F Major*

Ginastera, Alberto (1916-1983)

Country: Argentina
Known for: Nationalism
Recommended listening: *Suite de danzas criollas, Op. 15*

Górecki, Henryk (1933-2010)

Country: Poland
Known for: Spiritual minimalism
Recommended listening: *Symphony No. 3, Op. 36 (Symphony of Sorrowful Songs)*

Grainger, Percy (1882-1961)

Country: Australia
Known for: Folk-influenced
Recommended listening: *Molly on the Shore*

Griffes, Charles (1884-1920)

Country: USA
Known for: Impressionism
Recommended listening: *The Pleasure Dome of Kubla Khan, Op. 8*

Grofé, Ferde (1892-1972)

Country: USA
Known for: Nationalism
Recommended listening: *Grand Canyon Suite*

Hidas, Frigyes (1928-2007)

Country: Hungary
Known for: Folk-influenced wind music
Recommended listening: *Folksongs of the Balaton Suite*

Hindemith, Paul (1895-1963)

Country: Germany
Known for: Expressionism
Recommended listening: *Symphony in B-Flat Major*

Honegger, Arthur (1892-1955)

Country: Switzerland
Known for: Orchestral music
Recommended listening: *Rugby*

Hovhaness, Alan (1911-2000)

Country: USA
Known for: Orchestral music
Recommended listening: *And God Created Great Whales, Op. 229* (features the use of pre-recorded whale song)

Howells, Herbert (1892-1983)

Country: England
Known for: Sacred music
Recommended listening: *Hymnus Paradisi*

Husa, Karel (b. 1921)

Country: Czech Republic
Known for: Band music
Recommended listening: *Alto Saxophone Concerto*

Ibert, Jacques (1890-1962)

Country: France
Known for: Impressionism
Recommended listening: *Divertissement*

Ireland, John (1879-1962)

<u>Country:</u> England
<u>Known for:</u> Impressionism
<u>Recommended listening:</u> *Amberley Wild Brooks*

Ives, Charles (1874-1954)

- Three childhood memories greatly influenced Ives' music.
  1. As a child, he loved lying in bed at night with the window open so he could hear his father's band rehearsing in the town pavilion. Another band was also rehearsing at a nearby park, so Ives would hear two bands practicing two consonant pieces at the same time, which created a type of dissonant bitonality.
  2. Similarly, he also was fond of parades, particularly the sound of one marching band fading in the distance while another was approaching.[13]
  3. The sound of the less-skilled members of the congregation singing hymns in church, including their uneven rhythms and inaccurate pitches. Also, the sound of unison singing.[14]
- His career was as an insurance salesman, but he always composed as a hobby. At some point, he self-published his music and donated it to university music schools and performing arts organizations, and it started to be performed.[15]

<u>Country:</u> USA
<u>Known for:</u> Nationalistic orchestral music
<u>Recommended listening:</u> *Holidays Symphony*

---

13 Stuart Feder, *Charles Ives "My Father's Song": A Psychoanalytic Biography* (New Haven: Yale, 1992), 78–79.
14 J. Peter Burkholder, *Charles Ives and His World* (Princeton: Princeton, 1996), 8–9.
15 Stuart Feder, *The Life of Charles Ives* (Cambridge: Cambridge, 1999), 135–136.

Charles Ives' home in Danbury, Connecticut.

Jacob, Gordon (1895-1984)

<u>Country:</u> England
<u>Known for:</u> Chamber music
<u>Recommended listening:</u> *Sextet in B-Flat Major, Op. 6*

Janáček, Leoš (1854-1928)

<u>Country:</u> Czech Republic
<u>Known for:</u> Folk-influenced
<u>Recommended listening:</u> *Sinfonietta*

Kabalevsky, Dmitry (1904-1987)

<u>Country:</u> Russia
<u>Known for:</u> Neo-Romantic
<u>Recommended listening:</u> *The Comedians Suite, Op. 26*

Khachaturian, Aram (1903-1978)

<u>Country:</u> Armenia
<u>Known for:</u> Ballet

<u>Recommended listening</u>: *Spartacus*, especially "Adagio de Spartacus et Phrygie"

Kodály, Zoltán (1882-1967)

<u>Country</u>: Hungary
<u>Known for</u>: Folk-influenced
<u>Recommended listening</u>: *Hary Janos Suite*

Larsson, Lars-Erik (1908-1986)

<u>Country</u>: Sweden
<u>Known for</u>: Orchestral music
<u>Recommended listening</u>: *Sinfonietta for Strings, Op. 10*

Lehár, Franz (1870-1948)

<u>Country</u>: Hungary
<u>Known for</u>: Operetta
<u>Recommended listening</u>: *Das Land Des Lachelns*

Ligeti, György (1923-2006)

<u>Country</u>: Hungary
<u>Known for</u>: Avant-garde
<u>Recommended listening</u>: *6 Bagatelles*

Menotti, Gian Carlo (1911-2007)

<u>Country</u>: Italy
<u>Known for</u>: Opera
<u>Recommended listening</u>: *Amahl and the Night Visitors*

Messiaen, Olivier (1908-1992)

<u>Country</u>: France
<u>Known for</u>: Post-impressionism
<u>Recommended listening</u>: *Quartet for the End of Time*

Milhaud, Darius (1892-1974)

Country: France
Known for: Jazz-influenced
Recommended listening: *Le boeuf sur le toit, Op. 58*

Nordgren, Pehr (1944-2008)

Country: Finland
Known for: Nationalism
Recommended listening: *Portraits of Country Fiddlers, Op. 26*

Orff, Carl (1895-1982)

Country: Germany
Known for: Cantata
Recommended listening: *Carmina Burana*

Partch, Harry (1901-1974)

Country: USA
Known for: Avant-garde
Recommended listening: *8 Hitchhikers' Inscriptions*

Penderecki, Krzysztof (b. 1933)

Country: Poland
Known for: Avant-garde
Recommended listening: *Threnody to the Victims of Hiroshima*

Persichetti, Vincent (1915-1987)

Country: USA
Known for: Band music
Recommended listening: Parable No. 9, Op. 121

Piazzolla, Astor (1921-1992)

- He played the bandoneón, a type of squeeze-box accordion, and popularized its use in art music.
- As a teen, he had the opportunity to go on tour with a famous tango orchestra, but his father refused to let him go. This turned out to be a good thing, since the plane that was carrying the group crashed, killing everyone on board.[16]
- He studied composition in Paris with Nadia Boulanger who influenced him to find a unique voice. He achieved this by infusing his compositions with the tango and the bandoneón.[17]

<u>Country:</u> Argentina
<u>Known for:</u> Nationalism
<u>Recommended listening:</u> *Fuga y misterio*

Poulenc, Francis (1899-1963)

<u>Country:</u> France
<u>Known for:</u> Chamber music
<u>Recommended listening:</u> *Dialogues des Carmelites, FP 159*, especially the "Salve Regina" from Act III, scene 4 (opera)

Prokofiev, Sergei (1891-1953)

Sergei Prokofiev
Copyright in the Public Domain.

- His music is notable for its non-traditional melodies featuring huge interval leaps.
- composition *Peter and the Wolf* is often used by orchestras and chamber groups in concerts for younger children to help them get to know the different instruments of the orchestra, since each character in the story is represented by a different instrument: bird = flute; duck = oboe; cat = clarinet; bassoon = Grandfather; horn = wolf; and string instruments = Peter.[18]

<u>Country:</u> Russia

16   María Susana Azzi and Simon Collier, *Le Grand Tango: The Life and Music of Astor Piazzolla* (New York: Oxford, 2000), 16.
17   Natalio Gorin, Astor Piazzolla: A Memoir (Portland: Amadeus, 2001), 69.
18   Helen L. Kaufmann, The Story of Sergei Prokofiev (New York: Lippincott, 1971), 122.

<u>Known for:</u> Ballet
<u>Recommended listening:</u> *Cinderella*

Rachmaninoff, Sergei (1873-1943)

<u>Country:</u> Russia
<u>Known for:</u> Neo-Romantic
<u>Recommended listening:</u> *Piano Concerto No. 3 in D Minor, Op. 30*

Rautavaara, Einojuhani (1928-2016)

<u>Country:</u> Finland
<u>Known for:</u> Orchestral music
<u>Recommended listening:</u> *Cantus arcticus, Op. 61 (Concerto for Birds and Orchestra)*

Ravel, Maurice (1875-1937)

<u>Country:</u> France
<u>Known for:</u> Impressionism
<u>Recommended listening:</u> *Miroirs*

Respighi, Ottorino (1879-1936)

<u>Country:</u> Italy
<u>Known for:</u> Impressionism
<u>Recommended listening:</u> *The Pines of Rome*

Revueltas, Silvestre (1899-1940)

<u>Country:</u> Mexico
<u>Known for:</u> Nationalism
<u>Recommended listening:</u> *Homenaje a Federico Garcia Lorca*

Riegger, Wallingford (1885-1961)

<u>Country:</u> USA
<u>Known for:</u> Serialism
<u>Recommended listening:</u> *Concerto for Piano and Wind Quintet*

Rodrigo, Joaquin (1901–1999)

Country: Spain
Known for: Neo-Classical
Recommended listening: *Por los campos de Espana*

Roussel, Albert (1869–1937)

Country: France
Known for: Impressionism
Recommended listening: *The Spider's Banquet, Op. 17*

Satie, Erik (1866–1925)

Country: France
Known for: Avant-garde
Recommended listening: *Gymnopédies*

Schönberg, Arnold (1874–1951)

- His early compositions are highly Romantic in style.
- He invented the twelve-tone system to more easily compose atonal music.
- After receiving negative reactions from audiences regarding his and his students' music, he created the *Verein für musikalische Privataufführungen* (Society for Private Musical Performances). This was intended to keep people from booing or hissing at performances of new compositions. Among the rules of the society were 1) invited guests only and 2) no applause.[19]

Country: Austria
Known for: Serialism
Recommended listening: *Gurrelieder*

Shostakovich, Dmitri (1906–1975)

Country: Russia
Known for: Neo-Romantic
Recommended listening: *Symphony No. 6 in D Minor, Op. 47*

---

19 Joan Allen Smith, *Schoenberg and His Circle: A Viennese Portrait* (New York: Schirmer, 1986), 245–248.

Still, William Grant (1895-1978)

Country: USA
Known for: Nationalism
Recommended listening: *Symphony No. 1 "Afro-American"*

Stockhausen, Karlheinz (1928-2007)

Country: Germany
Known for: Electro-acoustic
Recommended listening: *Kontakte*

Stravinsky, Igor (1882-1971)

- At the premiere of *The Rite of Spring*, some members of the audience didn't like the music and began to boo and hiss. Other members of the audience liked the music and told the detractors to be quiet. One thing led to another, and it wasn't long before the audience devolved into a full riot.[20]
- When Disney made the animated movie *Fantasia*, they used *The Rite of Spring* for an extended sequence depicting prehistoric life and the demise of the dinosaurs.

A scene from Stravinsky's ballet *Firebird*.

---

20   Jonathan Cross, *Igor Stravinsky* (London: Reaktion, 2015), 48–52.

Stravinsky was quite upset that Disney hadn't depicted the actual story of the ballet, which involved pagan ritual and virgin sacrifice.[21]

Country: Russia
Known for: Ballet
Recommended listening: *Pulcinella*

Thomson, Virgil (1896–1989)

Country: USA
Known for: Opera
Recommended listening: *Four Saints in Three Acts*

Tomasi, Henri (1901–1971)

Country: France
Known for: Chamber music
Recommended listening: *Trois Divertissements*

Turina, Joaquín (1882–1949)

Country: Spain
Known for: Nationalism
Recommended listening: *Poema en forma de canciones, Op. 19*

Varèse, Edgard (1883–1965)

Country: France
Known for: Musique concrete
Recommended listening: *Poème Électronique*

Vaughan Williams, Ralph (1872–1958)

Country: England
Known for: Impressionism, Folk-influenced
Recommended listening: *The Lark Ascending*

---

21   Charles M. Joseph, *Stravinsky Inside* Out (New Haven: Yale, 2001), 110–111.

Villa-Lobos, Heitor (1887-1959)

Country: Brazil
Known for: Folk-influenced
Recommended listening: *Concerto for Guitar and Orchestra*

Walton, William (1902-1983)

Country: England
Known for: Neo-Romantic
Recommended listening: *Violin Concerto*

Webern, Anton (1883-1945)

- A student of Arnold Schönberg, he greatly admired serialism and even opined that the perfect piece of music would be one single statement of a twelve-tone row. As a result, most of his music is aphoristic (quite short).[22]
- He died after being shot by an American soldier during the occupation of Vienna following World War II. He had stepped out of his house after curfew to smoke a cigarette.[23]

Country: Austria
Known for: Aphoristic serialism
Recommended listening: *Three Little Pieces, Op. 11*

Anton Webern
Copyright in the Public Domain.

Weill, Kurt (1900-1950)

- He made political statements with his music, which caused him some problems with the Nazi party.[24]
- His music, both art music and popular (musical theatre), contain influences of jazz and folk music.

22 Hans Moldenhauer and Rosaleen Moldenhauer, *Anton von Webern: A Chronicle of His Life and Work* (New York: Knopf, 1979), 194.
23 Hans Moldenhauer, *The Death of Anton Webern: A Drama in Documents* (New York: Philosophical Library, 1961), 35.
24 Douglas Jarman, *Kurt Weill: An Illustrated Biography* (Bloomington: Indiana University Press, 1982), 64–65.

- Many of the arias and songs from his operas and musical theatre works have been recorded by jazz and pop artists all over the world.[25]

<u>Country:</u> Germany
<u>Known for:</u> Opera
<u>Recommended listening:</u> *Aufstieg und Fall der Stadt Mahagonny (The Rise and Fall of the City of Mahagonny)*, especially "Alabama Song" from Act I.

Wellesz, Egon (1885–1974)

<u>Country:</u> Austria
<u>Known for:</u> Orchestral music
<u>Recommended listening:</u> *Symphony No. 4, Op. 70 "Symphonia Austriaca"*

Xenakis, Iannis (1922–2001)

<u>Country:</u> Greece
<u>Known for:</u> Mathematical music
<u>Recommended listening:</u> *Metastaseis*

---

25   Stephen Hinton, *Weill's Musical Theater: Stages of Reform* (Los Angeles: University of California Press, 2012), 472.

CONTEMPORARY ERA (1960-PRESENT)

Most music history books group all of the music from 1900 to the present and call it the "Modern Era," but as each year passes, it becomes obvious that at some point the Modern Era needs to be divided up into more than one time period. In another 100 years or so, there will likely be a more obvious dividing line. For now, this book will take into consideration the composers who are still living today (or who were living until very recently), as well as the styles of the last fifty years or so, and call this time period—from 1960 onward—the Contemporary Era.

Instruments in the Contemporary Era

Instruments from previous time periods continue to be used and perfected today. In addition, new instruments are being invented.

Performance Venues in the Contemporary Era

The venues in the Contemporary Era are the same as in the Twentieth Century.

CHAPTER

TWENTY-TWO

Styles and Compositional and Performance Techniques of the Contemporary Era

Much of what was discussed in the chapters about the Twentieth Century applies equally to this time period. Most of the same styles and techniques continue to be used, including

- Impressionism
- Expressionism
- Nationalism
- Atonality/bitonality/polytonality
- Polyrhythm/polymeter/irregular meter/mixed meter
- Sprechstimme
- Serialism
- Indeterminacy/aleatory music/chance music
- Prepared piano
- Extended techniques
- Quoting/borrowing
- Electro-acoustic music

Style: Minimalism

Minimalism is another style that has its origins in the art world. Minimalist music features short motives, simple melodies, and simple harmonic progressions repeated over and over again. Minimalist music has a somewhat hypnotic effect as a result. In order to avoid a lapse into boredom, most minimalist composers will change a few notes or harmonies every few repetitions or so to keep things interesting.

There are sub-genres of minimalism called "Post-Minimalism" and "Holy" or "Spiritual Minimalism."

FURTHER INVESTIGATION:

Obtain a score of a minimalist composition by Terry Riley, Philip Glass, or Steve Reich and look at it to see if you can see the characteristics of minimalism.

SUGGESTED LISTENING:

- Terry Riley's *In C*
- Philip Glass' *String Quartet No. 2, "Company"*
- Steve Reich's *Nagoya Marimbas*
- John Adams' *Shaker Loops*
- Arvo Pärt's *Spiegel im Spiegel*

Compositional Technique: Phasing

Phasing is a technique in which two (or more) simultaneous performances of a melody, rhythm, or recorded sound fragment gradually get out of sync with each other. In other words, one performance is slightly (very slightly) faster than the other, so they "phase" out of sync, at first creating an echo effect, then, as the phase progresses, a rhythmic imitation, eventually phasing back into sync as the faster melody finally "catches up" with the slower melody.

FURTHER INVESTIGATION:

If you have good rhythm and a friend who also has good rhythm, get the score for Steve Reich's *Clapping Music* and try to perform it. It doesn't phase as gently as the suggested listening below, but it is still a good example of phasing.

SUGGESTED LISTENING:

- Matthew Burtner's *St. Thomas Phase*
- Steve Reich's *Piano Phase*
- Reich's *Phase Patterns*

CHAPTER
TWENTY-THREE
Genres of the Contemporary Era

Again, much of what was discussed in the chapters about the Twentieth Century applies equally to this time period. Most of the same genres continue to be popular.

Chamber Music

FURTHER INVESTIGATION:

1. Watch or listen to a piece of chamber music composed by a living composer.
2. Watch or listen to some Contemporary Era chamber music and some chamber music from an earlier time period. Note the stylistic differences.

SUGGESTED LISTENING:

- David Del Tredici's *Grand Trio*
- David Maslanka's *Wind Quintet No. 3*
- Pehr Henrik Nordgren's *String Quartet No. 10, Op. 142*

Pierrot Ensemble

SUGGESTED LISTENING:

- Joan Tower's *Petroushkates*
- Chen Yi's *... as like a raging fire ...*
- Ethan Wickman's *Winter's Burst*

Symphony

FURTHER INVESTIGATION:

1. Watch or listen to a symphony composed by a living composer.
2. Watch or listen to at least a half hour (each) of a Contemporary Era symphony and a symphony from an earlier time period. Note the stylistic differences.

SUGGESTED LISTENING:

- John Adams' *Son of Chamber Symphony*
- John Corigliano's *Symphony No. 3, "Circus Maximus"*
- David Maslanka's *Symphony No. 5*

Opera

FURTHER INVESTIGATION:

1. Watch an entire Contemporary Era opera. Many online sources have complete operas available for viewing, but make certain that you pick an option that has subtitles so you know what is going on. Alternatively, if subtitles are not provided, you can acquire a libretto (with the original text and an English translation) to follow along with.
2. Watch at least a half hour (each) of an opera from the Contemporary Era and an opera from an earlier time period. Note the stylistic differences.

SUGGESTED LISTENING:

- John Corigliano's *The Ghosts of Versailles*
- Steven Mackey's *Ravenshead*
- Daniel Catán's *Florencia en el Amazonas*

Concerto

FURTHER INVESTIGATION:

1. Watch or listen to a concerto composed by a living composer.
2. Watch or listen to a Contemporary Era concerto and a concerto from an earlier time period. Note the stylistic differences.

SUGGESTED LISTENING:

- Astor Piazzolla's *Bandoneon Concerto*
- Philip Glass' *Concerto for Saxophone Quartet*
- John Harbison's *Viola Concerto*

Mass

FURTHER INVESTIGATION:

1. Watch or listen to a Mass composed by a living composer.
2. Watch or listen to at least a half hour (each) of a Contemporary Era Mass and a Mass from an earlier time period. Note the stylistic differences.

SUGGESTED LISTENING:

- Roberto Sierra's *Missa Latina, "Pro Pace"*
- John Rutter's *Mass of the Children*
- David Maslanka's *Mass*

CHAPTER TWENTY-FOUR
Composers of the Contemporary Era

Adams, John (b. 1947)

- His operas have been somewhat controversial, particularly *The Death of Klinghoffer*—its subject matter involves a true story in which a group of Palestinians took a cruise ship hostage, ending with the death of a Jewish passenger who used a wheelchair.[1]

Country: USA
Known for: Opera, Minimalism
Recommended listening: *Nixon in China*

Bolcom, William (b. 1938)

Country: USA
Known for: Song cycle
Recommended listening: *Songs of Innocence and of Experience*

Corigliano, John (b. 1938)

Country: USA
Known for: Opera
Recommended listening: *The Ghosts of Versailles*

---

1   Edward W. Said, *Music at the Limits* (New York: Columbia, 2008), 134–139.

Del Tredici, David (b. 1937)

Country: USA
Known for: Rock-influenced avant-garde
Recommended listening: *Pop-Pourri*

Ferneyhough, Brian (b. 1943)

Country: England
Known for: Avant-garde
Recommended listening: *Unity Capsule*

Philip Glass at his piano.
Copyright © Pasquale Salerno (CC BY-SA 2.0) at https://commons.wikimedia.org/wiki/File:Philip_Glass_003.jpg.

Glass, Philip (b. 1937)

- With his chamber ensemble—the Philip Glass Ensemble—Glass was a musical guest on *Saturday Night Live* in 1986.
- He wrote the soundtracks for a trilogy of art films consisting entirely of images of day-to-day life, architecture, machinery, and technology. In order, the titles of the films in the trilogy are *Koyaanisqatsi, Powaqqatsi,* and *Naqoyqatsi.*[2]
- He has transitioned into film music and has been nominated for the Best Music Academy Award three times.

Country: USA
Known for: Minimalism
Recommended listening: *String Quartet No. 3, "Mishima"*

Harbison, John (b. 1938)

Country: USA
Known for: Neo-Romantic avant-garde
Recommended listening: *Ulysses' Bow*

---

2 Philip Glass, *Words Without Music*: A Memoir (New York: Liveright, 2015), 327–329.

Heggie, Jake (b. 1961)

Country: USA
Known for: Opera
Recommended listening: *Dead Man Walking*

Higdon, Jennifer (b. 1962)

Country: USA
Known for: Neo-Romantic
Recommended listening: *Percussion Concerto*

Maslanka, David (b. 1943)

- He spent twenty years as a faculty member at various schools before determining that, in order to truly achieve his desires as a composer, he had to believe in himself and not rely on a nine-to-five job. In 1990, he quit, moved to Montana, and became a freelance composer. He has made a living by composing ever since.
- He has embraced the Wind Ensemble (band) as a composition medium. He likes to write for bands because he feels they are more open to his music than orchestras.
- He believes strongly that composers need to achieve a meditative state at which point the music itself will tell the composer how to proceed.[3]

Country: USA
Known for: Neo-Romantic
Recommended listening: *Wind Quintet No. 2*

Muhly, Nico (b. 1981)

Country: USA
Known for: Avant-garde
Recommended listening: *Control (Five Landscapes for Orchestra)*

---

3 Timothy Salzman, ed. *A Composer's Insight: Thoughts, Analysis, and Commentary on Contemporary Masterpieces for Wind Band* (Galesville, MD: Meredith Music Publications, 2004), 95–98.

Pärt, Arvo (b. 1935)

Arvo Pärt

- Labeled as a Holy or Spiritual Minimalist, Pärt is known for works that consist of simple melodies and harmonies which move and evolve at a very slow pace. They have a hypnotic quality.[4]
- Before settling on his now distinctive style, he dabbled in serialism, aleatory works, and a technique he came up with called "collage technique," in which he borrowed fragments of well-known historical compositions and inserted them into the midst of his serialist compositions. (If interested, listen to *Collage sur BACH*.)[5]

<u>Country:</u> Estonia
<u>Known for:</u> Spiritual Minimalism
<u>Recommended listening:</u> *Fratres*

Reich, Steve (b. 1936)

- He used musique concrète in a unique way with his string quartet *Different Trains*. He interviewed a number of people who had experienced different kinds of trains (including his former nanny, a train conductor, and Holocaust survivors), then used fragments of their recorded voices to create melodies, replicating the pitch and rhythm of their speaking voices with the string instruments.[6]

<u>Country:</u> USA
<u>Known for:</u> Minimalism
<u>Recommended listening:</u> *Clapping Music*

Riley, Terry (b. 1935)

<u>Country:</u> USA
<u>Known for:</u> Minimalism
<u>Recommended listening:</u> *In C*

---

4   K. Robert Schwarz, *Minimalists* (London: Phaidon, 1996), 217.
5   Paul Hillier, *Arvo Pärt* (New York: Oxford, 1997), 47.
6   Thomas Rain Crowe, Rare Birds: *Conversations with Legends of Jazz and Classical Music* (Jackson: University Press of Mississippi, 2008), 129.

Rutter, John (b. 1945)

<u>Country:</u> England
<u>Known for:</u> Choral music
<u>Recommended listening:</u> *Requiem*

Rzewski, Frederic (b. 1938)

<u>Country:</u> USA
<u>Known for:</u> Avant-garde
<u>Recommended listening:</u> *Les Moutons de Panurge*

Saariaho, Kaija (b. 1952)

<u>Country:</u> Finland
<u>Known for:</u> Electro-acoustic
<u>Recommended listening:</u> *Nymphaea (Jardin secret III)*

Schwantner, Joseph (b. 1943)

<u>Country:</u> USA
<u>Known for:</u> Avant-garde
<u>Recommended listening:</u> *Aftertones of Infinity*

Sierra, Roberto (b. 1953)

Country: Puerto Rico
Known for: Nationalism
Recommended listening: *Trio No. 2*

Tavener, John (1944-2014)

Country: England
Known for: Spiritual Minimalism
Recommended listening: *Lament for Jerusalem*

Tower, Joan (b. 1938)

Country: USA
Known for: Avant-garde
Recommended listening: *Stroke*

Whitacre, Eric (b. 1970)

Country: USA
Known for: Choral music
Recommended listening: *Cloudburst*

Wuorinen, Charles (b. 1938)

Country: USA
Known for: Serialism
Recommended listening: *String Sextet*

Young, La Monte (b. 1935)

Country: USA
Known for: Minimalism
Recommended listening: *5 Small Pieces for String Quartet "On Remembering a Naiad"*

<u>Zwilich, Ellen Taaffe (b. 1939)</u>

<u>Country:</u> USA

<u>Known for:</u> Neo-Romantic

<u>Recommended listening:</u> *Peanuts Gallery* (a multi-movement work with each movement focusing on a different Peanuts character, including Charlie Brown and Snoopy)

SECTION 9

POPULAR MUSIC

As mentioned earlier in the book, the term "classical music" refers to all "art music" from the beginning of time to the present day and the term "pop music" refers to popular music of the twentieth and twenty-first centuries.

Some people have a hard time discerning the difference between pop and art music. This is certainly understandable because there are some grey areas where the two meet and overlap. Here are a few general considerations to keep in mind to help determine the difference between pop music and art music.

1. <u>Venue:</u> The location of the performance can sometimes help you determine if you are listening to art music or pop music. For instance, if you go to a public concert hall or an opera house, you are probably going to hear art music. If you go to a nightclub or arena, pop music is more likely.

2. <u>Product provided:</u> In the pop world, the product provided to the consumer is a very specific recording a particular artist made in a studio for the purpose of selling it. In the art music world, the product is the actual music score—the printed music. It is purchased by art musicians who then perform that music in live performances (and on recordings).

3. <u>Target audience:</u> The target audience for pop music is mostly young people who have the cash necessary to purchase the latest release by their favorite pop artists. On the other hand, the target audience for art music consists of people of all

ages who have developed a love of art music and want to enrich their lives by attending live performances and by listening to quality recordings.

4. <u>Type of publicity:</u> If your initial exposure to a particular musical artist was through a viral video, it's probably leaning more toward the "pop" side of things. If, instead, your initial exposure was at a concert, listening to an art music radio station, or attending a music history class, it's much more likely to be art music.

CHAPTER TWENTY-FIVE
Compositional and Performance Techniques of Popular Music

<u>Performance Technique: Covers</u>

A **cover** is when one pop artist records/performs another pop artist's song. The best covers are those in which something is changed to highlight the artist's qualities and to make the cover unique from the original.

FURTHER INVESTIGATION:

1. Watch a pop singing show or singing competition on television. Take note of the covers and notice the unique changes made to the original song.
2. Online, search for your favorite pop song to see if there are any covers of it. Compare and contrast the original with the covers.

SUGGESTED LISTENING:

There are literally hundreds of covers of songs by the Beatles. Listen to any of them.

<u>Performance Technique: Improvisation</u>

Improvisation has been around since the dawn of music. We've read about it already in the Baroque Era: cadenzas, basso continuo, da capo arias; in the Classical Era: cadenzas; in the Romantic Era: various character pieces that are supposed to sound improvised (even though they are not); and in the Twentieth Century: chance music.

Ella Fitzgerald, the undisputed queen of scat singing.

In popular music, improvisation shows up most frequently in jazz. Jazz musicians have trained their ears to follow the chord progressions played by the rhythm section and can improvise a melody based on the harmonic support. Interestingly, jazz is an area of music that still uses the modes that originated in the Middle Ages.

In "pop" music, singers often improvise elaborate melismas on a single note in a song. As an example, think of almost any performance of the national anthem you've ever heard by a pop star—lots of improvised melismas.

FURTHER INVESTIGATION:

1. Go to a live jazz performance. You'll see that various members of the jazz group will have a section within a piece of music to improvise for a while.

2. Listen to two different recordings of the same jazz standard. Note how the main melody is the same in both recordings, but the solo sections are radically different.

SUGGESTED LISTENING:

Live recordings of Benny Goodman, Miles Davis, or Charlie Parker.

Compositional Technique: Syncopation

Syncopation is a rhythm in which accented notes occur on unaccented beats or at unexpected times. It provides interest to a piece of music and is a common feature of rock-and-roll and jazz music.

Performance Technique: Scat-Singing

Scat-singing is when a singer improvises nonsense syllables instead of singing actual words.

SUGGESTED LISTENING:

Search online for videos of Ella Fitzgerald, Louis Armstrong, or Mel Tormé scat-singing.

Compositional Technique: Sampling

Popular music uses the technique of quoting/borrowing in some of the same ways, but the most common use of quoting/borrowing is a technique known as **sampling**. When a pop artist "samples" another artist's music, it is usually in the form of a musique concrète usage. Rap artists, for example, will take a preexisting pop song and sample a fragment of it and then repeat it over and over again as a bass line or accompaniment, while they rap on top of it.

FURTHER INVESTIGATION:

Search online for "pop music samples" or "sampling pop music" and you'll find plenty of examples.

SUGGESTED LISTENING:

- Original: "It's the Hard Knock Life" from *Annie*. Sample: *Hard-Knock Life* by Jay Z.
- Original: *Under Pressure* by Queen/David Bowie. Sample: *Ice, Ice Baby* by Vanilla Ice.
- Original: "The Lonely Goatherd" from *The Sound of Music*. Sample: *Wind It Up* by Gwen Stefani.

Performance Technique: Source Music

Source music (also known as **diegetic music**) is a technique used in film (or other theatrical presentation) in which the characters on screen provide music by singing/whistling/humming, attending a music performance, or turning on the radio or other sound device. In other words, the "source" of the music is on-screen.

FURTHER INVESTIGATION:

1. If you own any soundtracks, look at the listing of pieces/songs on the soundtrack. If there is a pop song listed and you can't recall hearing it, rewatch the movie to find out where it occurs—sometimes pieces of music are used for very short amounts of time. For instance, in some movies a character may be walking down the street and a car drives past with its stereo system blaring. That is source music.

2. Next time you watch a film, take note of any examples of source music.

Compositional Technique: Underscoring

Underscoring is the music in a movie (or other theatrical presentation) that "underscores" the action, or heightens the audience's experience by programmatically describing the visual action through music. This music is heard by the audience, but unheard by the characters on screen. If it were heard by the characters on screen, they would never go into those woods, or down that dark hallway, because the music would warn them not to. Underscoring can greatly affect the success of a movie. The most effective underscoring is relatively unobtrusive. If the viewer's mind is drawn away from the action on screen because of the music, the composer has not done his job well. Many soundtracks with underscoring also have leitmotivs.

FURTHER INVESTIGATION:

1. Search online for "worst soundtracks" and watch one of the films listed to see how horrible the underscoring is. (Keep in mind, this is in regard to instrumental/orchestral soundtracks—not soundtracks that consist entirely of pop music.)

2. Watch your favorite film and take note of how the underscoring affects your emotions.

CHAPTER TWENTY-SIX
Genres of Popular Music

Film Music

Film music, otherwise known as the "soundtrack," is a very important and influential popular genre. Film music can change the entire effect of a movie on the audience.

<u>Silent Films:</u> In the beginning days of film technology, films were completely silent. Audiences were so taken by the moving images, they didn't really care that they were sitting in silence. It didn't take too long for film-makers to realize that they could enhance their silent films with music. Theaters hired a local pianist or organist to improvise music that matched the mood or emotions of what was going on on-screen. As time went on, film-makers hired composers to write orchestral scores for the films. Then local theaters would hire a local orchestra to play the score while the movie was shown.

<u>Talkies:</u> When sound became a feature of film, initially film-makers felt that there was no need for a soundtrack because the audience could actually hear the actors—who needs music? But it didn't take long for music to return as a vital component of film-making.

Charlie Chaplin and Jackie Coogan in *The Kid*, a silent film.

FURTHER INVESTIGATION:

1. Watch a silent film, preferably in a theater with live keyboard accompaniment. Notice how the music is an attempt to match the emotions of the characters on screen.

2. Watch the original 1931 Hollywood production of "Dracula." The original had NO music (except for during the opening credits and closing credits). Then try to find the 1999 re-release of "Dracula" in which composer Philip Glass was commissioned to provide a soundtrack. There is a noticeable difference in how you feel while you watch the film.

Jazz

Louis Armstrong
Copyright in the Public Domain.

Jazz music is a style of music that has the following characteristics:

* Prominent use of improvisation
* Syncopation
* A featured soloist or soloists most often supported by a rhythm section (guitar and/or upright bass, keyboard, drum set) at the least, and a "big band" (a row of saxophones, a row of trombones, a row of trumpets, and rhythm section) at the most

Jazz evolved from a variety of sources:

* African work songs/slave songs
* African-American spirituals/gospel songs
* Post-slavery blues songs
* Rag-time piano music

Among the **many** varieties of jazz are the following:

* **New Orleans jazz**—small group of performers, usually featuring clarinet, trumpet, trombone, and rhythm section.
* **Swing** or "big band"—a large group of performers (as described above), often led by a featured performer on either a typical jazz instrument or voice.

- **Bebop**—started as a reaction against how commercial swing had become. Usually a trumpet or saxophone soloist supported by a small group of musicians (maybe two or three other instruments) and a rhythm section. Improvised solos in bebop tend to be quite fast and virtuosic.
- **Cool jazz**—a small ensemble with a variety of instruments. Cool jazz is relatively subdued, compared to the aggressive bebop style. Cool jazz pieces tend to be long and more "composed."
- **Jazz fusion**—jazz combined with pop or rock elements such as electric guitar and synthesizers.

All styles of jazz continue to flourish today in clubs and performance venues across the globe.

FURTHER INVESTIGATION:

1. Investigate the local nightclubs and bars to determine if any of them feature live jazz. In many cases, venues will specialize in a particular kind of jazz.
2. Listen to examples of each kind of jazz listed above to see if you can hear the differences.

SUGGESTED LISTENING:

- New Orleans jazz: *Indiana* performed by Louis Armstrong
- Swing: *Just Kiss Me* by Harry Connick, Jr.
- Bebop: *Confirmation* by Charlie Parker
- Cool jazz: *Take Five* by Dave Brubeck
- Jazz fusion: *Honky Tonk* by Miles Davis

Musical Theatre

Musical theatre is a story told through song, dance, and spoken dialogue. It is an American genre that owes at least some credit to opera, singspiel, and operetta (a light, comic opera). It also has its roots in vaudeville, a type of entertainment in early twentieth-century America that featured a variety of short performances from dancers, comedians, animal acts, and acrobats—a variety show. Performers in musical theater generally need to be what is called in the business a "triple threat," meaning that they need to be able to sing, dance, **and** act. There are many sub-genres within musical theatre, including:

- **Revues**—these shows are mainly a showcase for good songs; there is usually no storyline. Examples:
  - *Ziegfeld Follies of 1936*
  - *Side by Side by Sondheim*
  - *A Grand Night for Singing*
- **Book musicals**—This does not mean musicals based on novels (although it does not exclude them). A book musical is a musical with a clearly outlined narrative. The song and dance numbers grow out of the plot. Examples:
  - *The Sound of Music*
  - *Fiddler on the Roof*
  - *My Fair Lady*
- Operatic musicals—Musicals that do not have spoken dialogue but are entirely sung. Examples:
  - *Les Misérables*
  - *The Phantom of the Opera*
  - *Passion*
- Movie/TV adaptations—one trend for the past twenty years or so is reworking a movie (whether the movie was musical or not) into a stage production. Examples:
  - *Shrek the Musical*
  - *Spamalot* (based on "Monty Python and the Holy Grail")
  - *School of Rock*
- **Jukebox musicals**—storylines constructed using preexisting rock or pop songs. Examples:
  - *Mamma Mia* (using the music of ABBA)
  - *Rock of Ages* (pop hits of the 80's)
  - *American Idiot* (music of Green Day)

FURTHER INVESTIGATION:

Think of the musical theatre shows your high school produced and determine to which categories they belong.

Rock-and-Roll/Pop

Perhaps this is the broadest category of popular music. **Rock-and-roll** is a musical style that developed directly out of the blues. Early rock artists were blues artists who added a more driving rhythm and a heavier drum beat. **Pop** music means "popular" music. Sub-genres within the larger genre of rock-and-roll/pop include:

- Adult contemporary
- Alternative
- Bubblegum pop
- Christian rock
- Country-western
- Death metal
- Disco
- Doo wop
- Dubstep
- Folk rock
- Glam rock
- Grunge
- Heavy metal
- Hip-hop
- Indie rock

- K-pop
- Muzak
- New age
- Punk rock
- R&B
- Rap
- Reggae
- Rockabilly
- Ska
- Soft rock
- Surf music
- Techno
- Thrash
- Wizard rock
- Worldbeat

FURTHER INVESTIGATION:

1. Find an online music streaming site. Look at the searchable list of genres. Find five of the sub-genres listed above that you are not overly familiar with and listen to examples of them.
2. Borrow a friend's iPod/mp3 player to see what genres they have downloaded (with his/her permission, please).
3. Branch out of your comfort zone and listen to some styles that you haven't tried before.

CHAPTER

TWENTY-SEVEN
Composers of Popular Music

These, of course, are only partial lists of well-known composers of each genre.

Film Music Composers

COMPOSER	DATES	COUNTRY	FILM(S) BEST KNOWN FOR:
Arnold, Malcolm	1921–2006	England	*The Bridge on the River Kwai*
Bernstein, Leonard	1918–1990	USA	*On the Waterfront*
Copland, Aaron	1900–1990	USA	*The Heiress*
Corigliano, John	b. 1938	USA	*The Red Violin*
Elfman, Danny	b. 1953	USA	*Corpse Bride* *Edward Scissorhands* *Frankenweenie* *Nacho Libre* *The Nightmare Before Christmas* *Oz the Great and Powerful* *Pee-Wee's Big Adventure*
Giacchino, Michael	b. 1967	USA	*The Incredibles* *Mission: Impossible—Ghost Protocol* *Ratatouille* *Star Trek (2009)* *Up*
Glass, Philip	b. 1937	USA	*The Hours* *The Illusionist* *The Truman Show*

COMPOSER	DATES	COUNTRY	FILM(S) BEST KNOWN FOR:
Horner, James	1953-2015	USA	*The Amazing Spider-Man* *Avatar* *A Beautiful Mind* *Jumanji* *Titanic*
Newman, Thomas	b. 1955	USA	*Finding Nemo* *The Help* *The Shawshank Redemption* *Skyfall* *WALL-E*
Rota, Nino	1911–1979	Italy	*The Godfather*
Rozsa, Miklos	1907–1995	Hungary	*Ben-Hur* *Spellbound*
Shore, Howard	b. 1946	Canada	*The Hobbit* *Hugo* *The Lord of the Rings* *The Silence of the Lambs*
Williams, John	b. 1932	USA	*The Adventures of Tintin* *Close Encounters of the Third Kind* *E. T., the Extra-Terrestrial* *Harry Potter and the Sorcerer's Stone* *Home Alone* *Jaws* *Jurassic Park* *Lincoln* *Raiders of the Lost Ark* *Saving Private Ryan* *Schindler's List* *Star Wars*
Zimmer, Hans	b. 1957	Germany	*The Da Vinci Code* *The Dark Knight Rises* *Inception* *Kung Fu Panda* *The Lion King* *Madagascar* *Man of Steel* *Megamind* *Pirates of the Caribbean* *Sherlock Holmes*

Jazz Composers

COMPOSER	DATES	COUNTRY	GENRE
Armstrong, Louis	1901–1971	USA	New Orleans jazz, Swing
Basie, Count	1904–1984	USA	Swing
Beiderbecke, Bix	1903–1931	USA	New Orleans jazz
Blakey, Art	1919–1990	USA	Bebop
Brubeck, Dave	1920–2012	USA	Cool jazz
Coltrane, John	1926–1967	USA	Bebop
Corea, Chick	b. 1941	USA	Jazz fusion
Davis, Miles	1926–1991	USA	Bebop, Jazz fusion
Ellington, Duke	1899–1974	USA	Swing
Fitzgerald, Ella	1917–1996	USA	Scat-singing, Swing
Gillespie, Dizzy	1917–1993	USA	Bebop
Goodman, Benny	1909–1986	USA	Swing
Hancock, Herbie	b. 1940	USA	Bebop, Jazz fusion
Hawkins, Coleman	1904–1969	USA	Swing, Bebop
Holiday, Billie	1915–1959	USA	Vocal jazz
Marsalis, Wynton	b. 1961	USA	Jazz and Classical
Miller, Glenn	1904–1944	USA	Swing
Mingus, Charles	1922–1979	USA	Bebop
Monk, Thelonius	1917–1982	USA	Bebop
Morton, Jelly Roll	1890–1941	USA	New Orleans jazz, Swing
Mulligan, Gerry	1927–1996	USA	Cool jazz
Parker, Charlie	1920–1955	USA	Bebop
Prima, Louis	1910–1978	USA	Swing
Ra, Sun	1914–1993	USA	Jazz fusion
Roach, Max	1924–2007	USA	Bebop
Shaw, Artie	1910–2004	USA	Swing
Tatum, Art	1909–1956	USA	Solo piano
Waller, Fats	1904–1943	USA	Swing

Musical Theatre Composers

COMPOSER	DATES	COUNTRY	SHOWS BEST KNOWN FOR:
Berlin, Irving	1888–1989	Russia	*Annie Get Your Gun*
Bernstein, Leonard	1918–1990	USA	*On the Town* *West Side Story*
Bock, Jerry	1928–2010	USA	*Fiddler on the Roof*
Gershwin, George	1898–1937	USA	*Girl Crazy*
Hamlisch, Marvin	1944–2012	USA	*A Chorus Line*
John, Elton	b. 1947	England	*Aida* *Billy Elliot the Musical*
Kern, Jerome	1885–1945	USA	*Show Boat*
Larson, Jonathan	1960–1996	USA	*Rent*
Loewe, Frederick	1901–1988	Austria	*Brigadoon* *Camelot* *My Fair Lady*
MacDermot, Galt	b. 1928	Canada	*Hair*
Menken, Alan	b. 1949	USA	*Beauty and the Beast* *Little Shop of Horrors* *Newsies*
Porter, Cole	1891–1964	USA	*Anything Goes* *Kiss Me, Kate*
Rodgers, Mary	1931–2014	USA	*Once Upon a Mattress*
Rodgers, Richard	1902–1979	USA	*Carousel* *The King and I* *Oklahoma* *The Sound of Music* *South Pacific*
Schönberg, Claude-Michel	b. 1944	France	*Les Misérables* *Martin Guerre* *Miss Saigon*
Schwartz, Stephen	b. 1948	USA	*Godspell* *Pippin* *Wicked*
Shaiman, Marc	b. 1959	USA	*Hairspray*
Simon, Lucy	b. 1943	USA	*The Secret Garden*
Sondheim, Stephen	b. 1930	USA	*Assassins* *Into the Woods* *Pacific Overtures* *Sunday in the Park with George* *Sweeney Todd: The Demon Barber of Fleet Street*

COMPOSER	DATES	COUNTRY	SHOWS BEST KNOWN FOR:
Strouse, Charles	b. 1928	USA	*Annie* *Bye Bye Birdie*
Webber, Andrew Lloyd	b. 1948	England	*Cats* *Evita* *Jesus Christ Superstar* *Joseph and the Amazing Technicolor Dreamcoat* *The Phantom of the Opera*
Wildhorn, Frank	b. 1958	USA	*Jekyll & Hyde* *The Scarlet Pimpernel*
Willson, Meredith	1902–1984	USA	*The Music Man* *The Unsinkable Molly Brown*

INDEX

CPSIA information can be obtained
at www.ICGtesting.com
Printed in the USA
FSOW02n0347061217
42029FS